MW00773350

# THE BOUTIQUE

GREG ALEXANDER

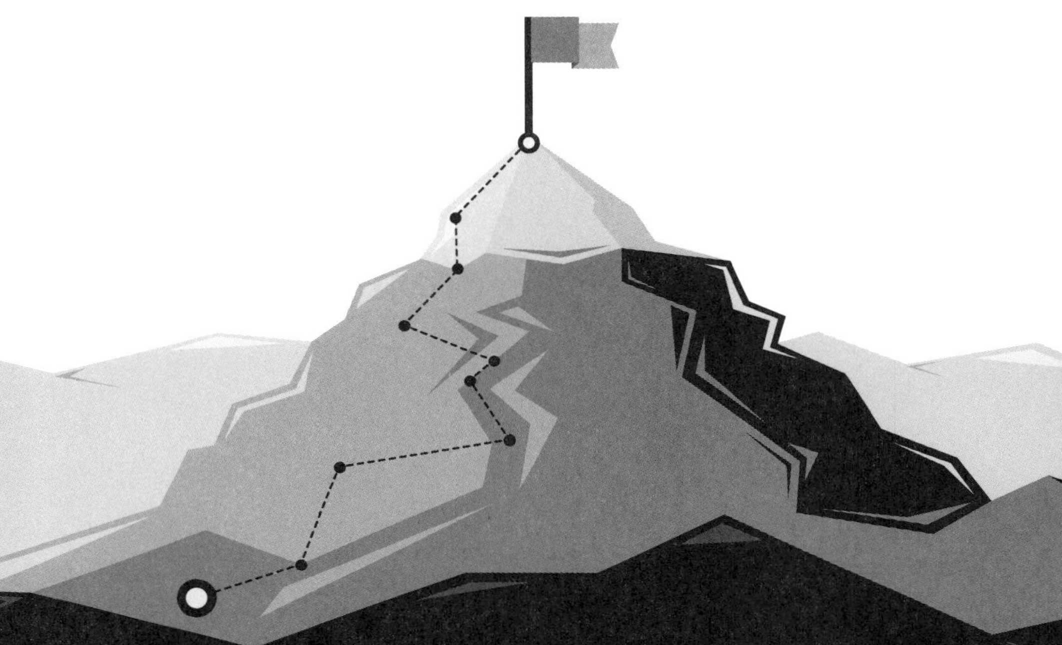

# THE BOUTIQUE

## HOW TO START, SCALE, AND SELL A PROFESSIONAL SERVICES FIRM

Advantage®

Published by Advantage, Charleston, South Carolina.
Member of Advantage Media Group.

ADVANTAGE is a registered trademark, and the Advantage colophon is a trademark of Advantage Media Group, Inc.

Printed in the United States of America.

10 9 8 7 6 5 4 3

ISBN: 978-1-64225-214-9
LCCN: 2020913723

Cover design by David Taylor.
Layout design by Megan Elger.

This publication is designed to provide accurate and authoritative information in regard to the subject matter covered. It is sold with the understanding that the publisher is not engaged in rendering legal, accounting, or other professional services. If legal advice or other expert assistance is required, the services of a competent professional person should be sought.

*To Woody, for teaching me that adding kindness to ability keeps you in the tall cotton.*

# CONTENTS

## SECTION 2: SCALE

## SECTION 3: SELL

# HOW TO READ THIS BOOK

The book is broken into three sections. It is not intended to be read sequentially. Each section is written for a specific audience. Pick the section(s) most interesting to you.

Section 1 is a guide for starting a boutique. It is relevant to readers who want to launch a new boutique.

Section 2 is a guide for scaling a boutique. It is relevant to readers who want to scale beyond a lifestyle business.

Section 3 is a guide for selling a boutique. It is relevant to readers who want to exit their boutiques.

In each section, there are chapters. Each chapter is intentionally short. These are guides, not scripts. At the end of each chapter, there is an exercise. The exercises consist of questions meant to stimulate new ways of thinking. All of the exercises are included in Appendix A, and a glossary of terms is included in Appendix B.

The chapters in the sections are also not meant to be read sequentially. Think of them like recipes in a cookbook. Pick the section(s) and then the chapter(s) most relevant to you. Each stands on its own.

Lastly, the book is short for a reason. There are those of you who will want to read all of it. All the blah, blah, blah is stripped away. You can read it in less time than it takes to watch a movie.

# FOREWORD

This book will make you a better leader of your professional services firm. It will challenge you to think, and it will confront some beliefs you have. It is hard hitting. It is real.

Greg's approach will help you avoid common pitfalls, allowing you to build wealth quickly.

I can say this with certainty because I have seen Greg accomplish these things. More than that, I can say this with conviction. I left my position as president of YPO, and I joined Greg as the CEO of Capital 54. I did so because I share his view that we are in the golden era of boutiques. And I want to be a part of it.

I have joined Greg to give back by helping you accomplish your most audacious goals—practically, carefully, and with intent.

I have been working in the professional services arena for over thirty years. I have had the amazing good fortune to observe some of the most accomplished CEOs in the world. Greg is a leader among these leaders. He is real, he is an unfiltered learner, and he walks the talk.

Greg and I are both members of a global peer organization called YPO. And both of us qualified for our membership by growing and scaling professional services firms.

I led YPO as its global president and COO for over seven years. I also helped build The Entrepreneurs' Organization, EO, with sixteen years of volunteer contributions and a seven-year stint on their board. Prior to this, I started and sold three firms. I share this with you for context. I have had the benefit of thirty years of being an owner, and working with owners, across industries in over 130 countries.

As you can imagine, I have experienced successes and failures. I have seen quite a few very well-earned exits. In all cases I have observed that leaders of successful firms have three things in common: a well-honed ability to thrive on constant change, a mastery of ambiguity, and the ability to synthesize data from trusted sources. There are many more factors at play, but these are a constant.

In this easy-to-read and practical book, you will learn to constantly ask the most uncomfortable and challenging questions: Where will my business be in three, four, five years? Will it succeed in its chosen field, or will it just be a middle-of-the-pack player? Where is my firm headed now, and how will I know it is on the right path?

I wish I had met Greg years ago. The lessons shared here would have saved me a great deal of time, pain, and money.

Although our journeys have been different, our experiences have generated similar lessons and understandings.

This book does not present all the answers, as no book could. It provides a framework in the three distinct areas of starting, scaling, and selling a boutique.

This book will help you make fast and accurate assessments on what your real opportunities are without getting bogged down in detail. It will force you to think for yourself. If you only get to answer three questions from exploring these pages, answer these: What do you really want? What is factual and real? What are you going to do about it?

It matters who you ask questions and take advice from. Listening to uninformed, untested, and inexperienced people is worse than not having any advice at all. That is the beauty of peer organizations like YPO and Collective 54.

Within the ranks of Collective 54 are battle tested, fully informed people in every aspect of starting, scaling, and selling professional services firms. When asked with humility, these peers will share straight facts with you. They may even be future customers, partners, acquirers, and mentors. My own experience as a member of Collective 54, benefitting my former role and impact at YPO, speaks for itself.

Greg and I share a common mantra: find out who is responsible for whatever it is we are seeking to learn and understand and then ask them. This approach can raise a firm's performance by an order of magnitude and deliver real, sustainable growth and fulfill your dreams. Businesses within the professional services sector face very similar issues, regardless of the niche they are in.

If you do read this book, I hope that you reflect on the questions and experiences in its pages.

Weigh them for yourself and decide if and how you can use them to help you achieve your goals.

If you are challenged by what you read and you want to discuss it with someone or you want access to independent thinkers who are your peers on a similar journey, come and join us at Collective 54.

Thank you, Greg, for your candor, your inspiration, your resilience, and your commitment to our industry. I love this journey we are on!

**Sean Magennis**
CEO of Capital 54, former president of YPO and former president of EO

# PREFACE

In 2017, I sold my consulting firm for nine figures and retired.

My wife and I then spent the next two and a half years traveling the world.

In early 2020, a global pandemic called COVID-19 started killing thousands. My retirement was interrupted as travel was banned. As the weeks passed, my telephone began to ring. Friends and colleagues, whom I had lost touch with, started to reconnect. Boredom had set in. People needed something to do. Reconnecting with old friends took up the time.

During these calls, I would share what I had been up to. The Sales Benchmark Index (SBI) story was not well known. My firm was in an obscure cottage industry and was not a brand anyone would recognize. Once they heard the story, I kept getting asked, "How did you pull that off?" Some would say, "You should write a book."

So, sheltered in place and tired of watching TV, I began writing. This is how this book came about.

I am writing this book for owners' boutique professional services firms. If you are trying to start, scale, or sell a boutique, this is for you. I want to help you realize your dreams. My dreams have come true, and it is time to give back. I have learned a few things and want to share.

You should know that there is nothing special about me. I came from a middle-class family. I went to public schools and universities. I have an average IQ and a below-average EQ. What I do have, however, is specific tribal knowledge in this field. I acquired this knowledge firsthand. I started at my kitchen table with an idea. Ten years later, I took it all the way to the bank. If I can do it, so can you. I hope this book inspires you to go for it.

# INTRODUCTION

What is a boutique professional services firm?

According to the government, a professional services firm is in industry code NAICS 54. Examples are firms in consulting, accounting, law, marketing and advertising, architecture, engineering, and so on. Basically, anyone who sells their expertise.

There are approximately 1.47 million firms like this in the United States. 4,100 have reached scale, which is defined as those with more than 250 employees. This is one-quarter of 1 percent. These are called market leaders.

The other 1,465,900, or 99.75 percent, have between 1 and 249 employees. These are called boutiques.

This book is for the boutiques. It is about what the market leaders, or the one-quarter of 1 percent, did to scale. It is about what the boutiques, or the 99.75 percent, need to do to scale. And this gap between doing and not doing makes all the difference.

Do you need to be convinced?

Try this on for size. Each year $2 trillion is spent in this sector. The top one-quarter of the 1 percent, the 4,100, capture most of it. If you want a bigger piece of the pie, you need to scale.

Why should you listen to me?

I think I am worth listening to for three reasons.

I have firsthand experience in this field. I started, scaled, and sold a boutique for nine figures in ten years. I did what you are trying to do.

I own the leading investment firm in this category, Capital 54. It provides capital exclusively to boutiques. I do not just write and talk about this subject. I put my money were my mouth is. I place large bets on my ideas.

I also own the national peer-to-peer membership network for boutiques, Collective 54. In practical terms, this means that I have a direct line to the practitioners. My ideas are not academic. They are sourced directly.

I hope my credentials have established my credibility on this subject.

Why this book at this moment in time?

I believe that we are in the golden era of boutiques. The business models of your clients are being disrupted. This makes it virtually impossible for them to have all the required expertise in-house. They are looking for external expertise. They have big budgets to spend. Clients are turning to boutiques in record numbers. They want specialists and have grown tired of generalists.

The sun is shining. Time to make hay.

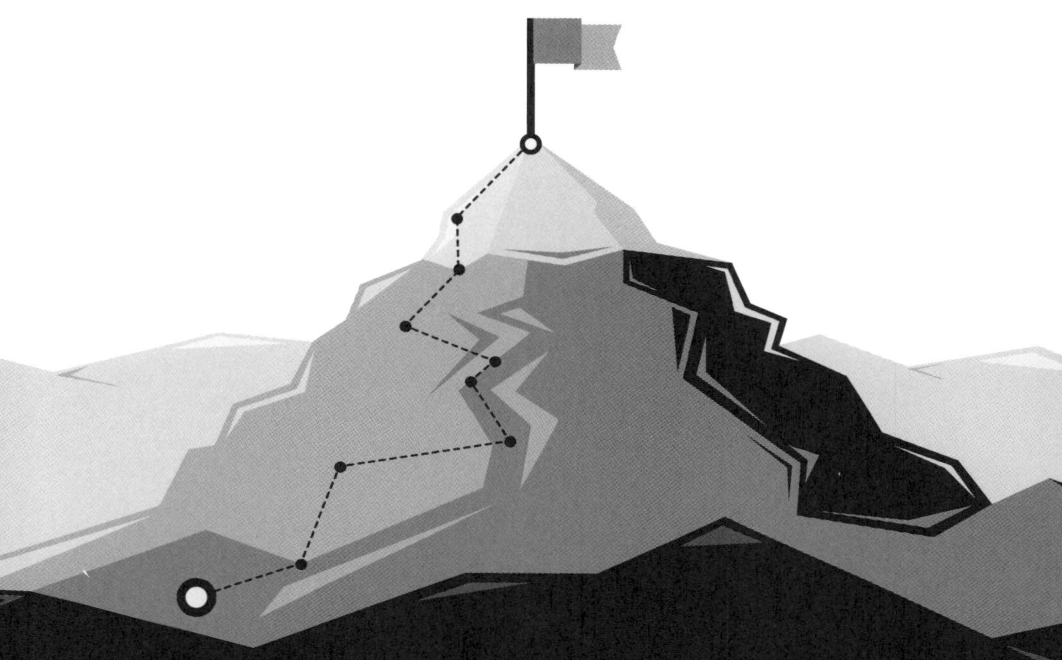

SECTION 1

# START

## CHAPTER 1

# THE PROBLEM

When starting a boutique, it is best to begin with the problem you will solve for clients. Why? There are lots of boutiques with solutions that no one is going to buy. The idea you have for your firm is valid if you can do the following:

- State the problem you solve for clients.
- Determine that the problem is pervasive.
- Confirm that clients will be willing to pay to solve it.
- Prove that the problem is urgent.

> **When starting a boutique, it is best to begin with the problem you will solve for clients.**

An entrepreneur recently came to Capital 54 looking for investment capital. He had an idea for a boutique. He was seeking start-up capital to hire the staff, develop the service, and take it to market. He explained his solution elegantly. He was clearly a domain expert. His field of expertise was price optimization in the information security business.

I asked him to explain the problem that the target client was experiencing. He answered by telling me that the clients were unaware of the problem they had. The problem was demand curve modeling. He was going to bring it to their attention. His target clients did not know they had a problem. Strike one.

I then asked how many clients had this problem. He answered, "All of them." He showed me that there were approximately ten thousand information security companies that need price optimization. He stated that he would reach 1 percent market share by end of year three, resulting in one hundred clients. He suggested that each client was going to pay $250,000. This meant that his three-year revenue projections were $25 million. He assumed that every company in the sector had the problem. Strike two.

My colleague chimed in. He asked if he had confirmed that clients were willing to pay $250,000 to solve this problem. This would-be entrepreneur shared with us a price list from competitors in the space. He stated that clients would hire him because he was 20 percent less.

My colleague then asked if this was an urgent problem or a nice-to-have. This person explained that it is not urgent, but it should be. Therefore, he did not know whether the client was willing to pay to solve the problem. And he did not know whether the problem was urgent. Strike three.

I share this story to save you from making the same mistakes. Starting a boutique is hard. In the early days, you will be working for free. You will be burning through whatever cash you have until clients start paying you. You cannot afford to waste time evangelizing a solution. You need to generate paying clients as quickly as possible.

Be in the painkiller business. Do not be in the vitamin business. Why do more people buy painkillers than vitamins? When you are in pain, it is urgent. You are willing to pay to make the pain stop now. Be sure that your solution addresses a real problem, that the problem is urgent, and that people are willing to pay to solve it.

How?

Here is a ten-question exercise to use:

1. When you explain the problem to your family, do they understand you?

   ☐ yes ☐ no
2. When you explain the problem to friends, do they understand you?

   ☐ yes ☐ no
3. Does the problem exist in more than one industry?

   ☐ yes ☐ no
4. Does the problem exist in companies of all sizes?

   ☐ yes ☐ no
5. Does the problem exist in many geographies?

   ☐ yes ☐ no
6. Are clients paying to solve the problem today?

   ☐ yes ☐ no
7. Have clients been paying to solve this problem for years?

   ☐ yes ☐ no
8. If clients do not solve the problem, are the consequences severe?

   ☐ yes ☐ no
9. Is there a trigger event that puts clients in the market for your solution?

   ☐ yes ☐ no

10. When clients have the problem, do they work to get it solved by a deadline?

    ☐ yes ☐ no

If you answered no to eight or more of these questions, you do not have a problem worth solving. Your task is to adjust your problem statement to convert the nos to yeses.

If you answered yes to eight or more of these questions, you have a problem worth solving. This gives you an indication to move on to the next step.

## SUMMARY

Start with the problem you will solve for clients. Be sure that it is easy to understand and that many clients are experiencing it. And be sure that clients are willing to pay to solve it. Lastly, ensure that the problem is urgent and is one that the client cannot ignore.

## CHAPTER 2

# THE CLIENT

Socrates once said, "Know thyself." If he were alive today and leading a boutique, he would say, "Know thy client." It is harder to sell a service than it is to sell a product. A service is an intangible that makes it harder for clients to buy it. Therefore, understanding your client takes on significance when starting a boutique. The better you understand your client, the better you can serve them.

You know who your client is if you can produce two things:

1. A demographic profile
2. A psychographic profile

A demographic profile includes items such as the following:

- Race
- Ethnicity
- Gender
- Age
- Education
- Industry

- Title
- Role
- Income level
- Location
- And more

A psychographic profile includes items such as the following:

- Wants
- Needs
- Desires
- Goals
- Emotions
- Values
- Attitudes
- Interests
- Challenges
- Priorities
- And others

I recently spoke with a professional translator. He has a unique service delivery model. He leverages technology that allows him to deliver a project in half the time. This person is a one-man shop, and he wants to build a firm. When I asked him, "Who is the client?" his answer was incomplete. He described the client as software publishers looking to expand internationally. This is a description of a company and a thin one at that. Services are bought by people. I encouraged him to get into the hearts and minds of the client.

This would involve understanding the motives of the client. Why was this person put in charge of selecting a translation service? Were they confident that they could select the right one? Is the client impatient, or are they going to take their time researching? Are they knowledgeable in this field? Or are they doing this for the first time? Was their career at risk if they made the wrong decision? Were they concerned about how their boss would react to who they picked?

These are some of the types of questions you need answers to. Launching a boutique without a deep understanding of the client is a costly mistake. It will result in wasting time and money on failed attempts to acquire clients. Your message will not resonate with the target client.

**Launching a boutique without a deep understanding of the client is a costly mistake.**

Want to get started?

Here are the yes/no questions for this chapter:

1. Do you have a demographic profile for your target client?

   ☐ yes ☐ no

2. Do you have a psychographic profile for your client?

   ☐ yes ☐ no

3. Do you have an elevator pitch that speaks directly to the client?

   ☐ yes ☐ no

4. Do you understand the personal goals of the client?

   ☐ yes ☐ no

5. Do you understand the professional goals of the client?

   ☐ yes ☐ no

6. Do you understand the obstacles preventing the client from accomplishing the personal goals?

   ☐ yes ☐ no

7. Do you understand the obstacles preventing the client from accomplishing the professional goals?

   ☐ yes ☐ no

8. Do you understand the likely objections that your client is going to submit to you?

   ☐ yes ☐ no

9. Do you understand the client's top priorities?

   ☐ yes ☐ no

10. Do you understand the emotional makeup of the client?

    ☐ yes ☐ no

If you answered no to eight or more of these questions, you are not ready to launch a boutique. The task would be to speak to as many potential clients as you can. Your research should be primary, meaning that you personally interview these people. Firsthand direct knowledge is the key.

If you answered yes to eight or more of these questions, you understand your client. The task is to document it in a demographic and psychographic profile. These profiles will be used by everyone every day.

## SUMMARY

Know thy client. Get inside their hearts, souls, and minds. Try to know them better than they know themselves. Take this knowledge and drive it into everything you do. When a prospective client bumps into you, they should say, "These people get me."

CHAPTER 3

# THE COMPETITORS

There are five types of competitors for all boutiques. They are as follows:

1. Do nothing
2. Internal resources
3. Boutiques
4. Market leaders
5. Other

Approximately 40 percent of the time you will be competing with "do nothing." This competitor can be described as the project that went away. The client did not hire you or one of your competitors. They just decided not to go forward with the initiative. The reason this happens about 40 percent of the time is that you are not pursuing the urgent. The client has other priorities.

The way to defeat "do nothing" is to calculate the cost of inaction. You need to prove to the client that your project deserves their full attention. It is the priority. As they say, "Money talks and BS walks." Put a hard dollar on their inaction, and you will defeat this competitor.

Approximately 30 percent of the time you will be competing with internal resources. These clients think that they can do what you can do. And they think that they can do it better than you and for "free." The reason this happens about 30 percent of the time is that there is no compelling event. The client is not concerned with how long the project takes. There is no deadline breathing down their necks.

The way to defeat internal resources is to establish a deadline. Explain to the client that completing the project inside of this deadline is very difficult. It is too risky for them to try to do so on their own. Share with the client the true workload. Make it obvious that they need help.

Approximately 20 percent of the time you will be competing with other boutiques. Highly specialized prescale firms are very attractive to potential clients. The reason this happens about 20 percent of the time is that some clients have budget constraints. They turn to boutiques because, in general, boutiques are less costly.

The way to defeat boutique competitors is to guarantee the work. Boutiques have limited resources, and this makes them risk averse. The idea of a guarantee frightens them, as they may not get paid. By guaranteeing your work, you separate yourself from the boutique competitors.

**By guaranteeing your work, you separate yourself from the boutique competitors.**

Approximately 5 percent of the time you will be competing with the market leaders. These are the 4,100 firms that have scaled to more than 250 employees. The reason this happens only about 5 percent of the time is that most boutiques are not in these deals.

Clients who can afford the market leaders tend not to ask boutiques to bid. However, when they do, these deals represent the year makers. Therefore, boutiques must be excellent at beating the market leaders. Although it is only 5 percent of the pipeline, these are the big deals. Just one or two wins per year can mean a lot.

The way to defeat the market leaders is by implementing a five-step approach. Step one is to establish your credibility. Prove to the client that you are worthy of consideration. Step two is to deliver a top-quality proposal. This will signal to the client that you deliver exceptional work. Step three is to demonstrate to the client that you can complete the work much faster. The advantage of a boutique is speed. Big firms can be very slow moving. Step four is to offer the same quality of work for 25 percent less cost. Market leaders are expensive. They can be defeated with competitive pricing. Don't discount too much, for it may mistakenly signal that you are "cheap." Step five is to offer an enjoyable experience. Market leaders enter a client like a tornado and are very disruptive. The advantage of working with a boutique is that they are easier to deal with.

Approximately 5 percent of the time you will be competing with "other." This is to say that you are competing with alternative ways of solving the client's problem. The two most common "others" are executive search and software providers. Clients often think that the fast way to solve a problem is to fire someone. This is quickly followed by hiring a replacement. In other cases, clients think that they can license a piece of software and the problem goes away.

The way to defeat "other" is to perform a postmortem. The postmortem highlights that the last time they took this approach, it did not work. For instance, the hiring error rate is high, especially so at the executive level. And many software applications have low user adoption rates. Once the client is reminded of these previous attempts, they typically eliminate them.

Here are this chapter's yes/no questions:

1. Can you calculate a client's cost of inaction?

   ☐ yes ☐ no

2. Can you find a compelling event that puts a deadline on the client's project?

   ☐ yes ☐ no

3. Are you confident enough to guarantee your work?

   ☐ yes ☐ no

4. Can you establish your credibility in the eyes of your client?

   ☐ yes ☐ no

5. Can you signal quality to the client by delivering a best-in-class proposal?

   ☐ yes ☐ no

6. Can you deliver much faster than the market leaders in your niche?

   ☐ yes ☐ no

7. Can you earn healthy margins and still be 25 percent less than the market leaders?

   ☐ yes ☐ no

8. Are you more enjoyable to work with than the market leaders?

   ☐ yes ☐ no

9. Do you understand the alternative solutions to the problem you address?

   ☐ yes ☐ no

10. Will a postmortem reveal to the client that these alternatives have a poor track record?

    ☐ yes ☐ no

If you answered no to eight or more of these questions, you are not ready to compete. The task is to prepare for competition by converting the nos to yeses.

If you answered yes to eight or more of these questions, you are ready to win. The task is to get in as many deals as possible. Your win rate will be very high.

## SUMMARY

A start-up boutique must win a high percentage of the time. They are not in enough deals to allow for many deals to be lost. No one wins every deal. But that should be the goal. By establishing a competitive playbook, you can make sure to beat the other guys consistently.

CHAPTER 4

# THE REVENUE

The sources of revenue available to boutiques are most often as follows:

- Hourly billings
- Retainers
- Fixed bids
- Performance-based contracts
- Memberships
- Licensing
- Subscriptions
- Events
- Royalties

It is important for a boutique to think through the right mix for them. Going to market with a single source of revenue is a common mistake. Avoid this mistake by considering these nine revenue sources.

Charging clients an hourly rate has the benefit of being easy to implement. However, it limits the amount of revenue you can generate. There is a fixed number of hours. There is an upper limit on how much you can charge for each hour.

A retainer is when a client pays you up front to secure your services when needed. This has the benefit of getting paid in advance and of predictable cash flow. However, there are only so many retainers that a boutique can handle at one time.

A fixed-bid project is using a flat amount regardless of the number of hours worked. This is profitable work for boutiques if they can scope projects correctly. Clients are buying a deliverable, not the boutique's time. If the boutique can produce the deliverable efficiently, this is very profitable.

A performance-based contract aligns the client's and the boutique's interests. If the boutique produces a result, they get paid. If they fail, they do not get paid. Boutiques can capture a lot of upside revenue with performance-based contracts. They are usually uncapped. However, boutiques can lose a lot of revenue if they do not produce.

**Boutiques can capture a lot of upside revenue with performance-based contracts.**

A client pays a boutique a membership fee if they want to belong to a group. The annual dues grant a client access to a group of like-minded peers. Some boutiques include access to their clients as part of their value proposition.

A licensing fee is paid by a client to a boutique for use of intellectual property. Many boutiques have methodologies and tools that clients want unlimited access to. They pay a licensing fee for the right to use them as they see fit.

A subscription is paid by a client to a boutique to gain access to an asset. For example, many boutiques have proprietary data. Clients want access to this data and pay a subscription to a database.

Boutiques often put on events and conferences. Clients pay a boutique for a ticket, or tickets, to be granted admission to the event.

Some boutiques are paid royalties from other boutiques. This happens when a boutique wants to use someone else's intellectual property but pay on performance. For instance, a sales training firm allows a distributor to use their training material. When the distributor signs an engagement, they pay the training firm a royalty.

Not knowing any better, early on, my boutique generated revenue with hourly billings. As I grew, I bumped into the limitations of this revenue approach. I added fixed bids to the mix. I lost my shirt the first few times. I was inexperienced in defining scope. Clients took advantage of us. As we got better, we shifted more work to fixed bids. Profitability increased. Clients would pay us for a list of deliverables. As we became efficient at producing them, costs went down while prices stayed fixed. Things got interesting when we added performance-based fees to the mix. In our market, project success was measured by revenue per sales head. Clients would hire us to improve this metric. This meant generating more revenue for clients while not adding sales reps. We stopped charging clients fees but asked for a percentage of the gain. These projects became the home runs. We had to be careful where and when to use performance-based fees. But, when done correctly, it was very lucrative. Our mix evolved into one-third retainers, one-third fixed bids, and one-third performance-based fees, or thereabouts.

Which of these do you want to start with? What is the right mix for you?

This chapter's questions will help you think through this.

1. Will a client pay you more than $500 per hour?

   ☐ yes ☐ no

2. Will a client pay you in advance to secure your service on demand?

   ☐ yes ☐ no

3. Can you scope your projects with precision?

   ☐ yes ☐ no

4. Can you prove direct attribution of results in your engagements?

   ☐ yes ☐ no

5. Will your clients pay you for the privilege of speaking to your other clients?

   ☐ yes ☐ no

6. Will your clients pay you for the right to use your intellectual property?

   ☐ yes ☐ no

7. Do you have proprietary data that clients would like to subscribe to?

   ☐ yes ☐ no

8. Do you put on events, and are clients willing to buy tickets to attend?

   ☐ yes ☐ no

9. Are other boutiques willing to pay you a royalty to distribute your intellectual property?

   ☐ yes ☐ no

10. Does your business model include at least three sources of revenue?

    ☐ yes ☐ no

Each of these questions maps to the nine sources of revenue. For instance, question 1 maps to revenue source 1 and so on. If you answer yes to a question, you should consider this a revenue source. If you answer no, you should not. Question 10 does not map to a specific revenue source. It is focused on eliminating the risk of a single revenue source. The rule of thumb is to launch a boutique with at least three revenue sources.

## SUMMARY

There are many different sources of revenue available to boutiques. You have a deep understanding of the problem you solve. You understand intimately who you solve it for. And you can articulate why you are the best person to solve it. Turn your attention to the monetization strategy. Develop a mix of revenue sources that pay you fairly for the value you deliver.

CHAPTER 5

# THE SERVICE

A few months ago, I met a brilliant bookkeeper. She developed a way for small business owners to outsource bookkeeping for $9.99 per month. It was a smart combination of technology automation and offshore labor. Her competitors charged hundreds of dollars per month for a similar service. She is doubling her revenue and profit every year. I tried to invest in her company, but she did not need me. I call her the one that got away.

I learned some valuable lessons from her that I would like to share.

The first lesson is to be imaginative as to how you deliver your service. Many boutiques are conventional in their approach. They convert their expertise into a methodology and train staff members how to use it. At times, more often than not, they use expensive labor and very little automation. As a result, their service is expensive and tough to sell. This constrains their growth.

The second lesson is that commodity services are ripe for disruption. Prior to meeting her, I would not have believed that bookkeeping is a growth industry. And if you look at the numbers in the aggregate, it is not. However, there were 183,077 bookkeeping firms in the United States in 2019. The average cost of an in-house bookkeeper is $40,831 per year. My friend has reduced this to $119 per year. The bookkeeping industry might not be growing, but she is. In fact, she is shooting ducks in a barrel.

The third lesson is that clients hire boutiques for one of three reasons. First, you can do what they can do better. Second, you can do what they can do faster. Third, you can do what they can do cheaper. Ideally, you combine better, faster, and cheaper into a single value proposition. And when I say better/faster/cheaper, I mean in relation to the alternatives. In chapter 3, we learned that there are five alternatives: (1) do nothing, (2) internal resources, (3) boutiques, (4) market leaders, and (5) other.

The fourth lesson is that there is a lot of money to be made in boring areas. Before you chase the next hot thing, remember what Sam Walton said: "If you want to dine with the classes, you better sell to the masses."

Our technology-obsessed culture pushes you toward chasing the shiny new field. If I hear one more pitch on AI, I am going to jump out my window. However, there are 254,611 architectural firms in the US, 83,712 landscaping businesses in our great country, and 34,832 interior design firms, just to name a few examples. You do not need to be the next Einstein to realize your dreams.

As you think through your boutique's service offering, consider this chapter's questions:

1. Are you offering a service that clients are already buying?

   ☐ yes ☐ no

2. Are there many legacy firms providing this service?

   ☐ yes ☐ no

3. Are these legacy firms ripe for disruption?

   ☐ yes ☐ no

4. Can you use less expensive labor to deliver it?

   ☐ yes ☐ no

5. Can you use technology automation to streamline it?

   ☐ yes ☐ no

6. Can you perform the service better than the alternatives?

   ☐ yes ☐ no

7. Can you perform the service faster than the alternatives?

   ☐ yes ☐ no

8. Can you perform the service cheaper than the alternatives?

   ☐ yes ☐ no

9. Can you combine better/faster/cheaper into a single value proposition?

   ☐ yes ☐ no

10. Are you staying away from the latest fad that might not have staying power?

   ☐ yes ☐ no

If you answered yes to eight or more of these questions, you will bring a winning service to market. The task is to get it to market quickly while it has an advantage.

If you answered no to eight or more of these questions, your service will be hard to sell. The task is to reengineer it in such a way to make it more distinctive.

## SUMMARY

Entrepreneurs often don't put innovation and service in the same sentence. Boutiques do not look at themselves as disruptors. The innovator label is most often only applied to leaders of product companies. Yet the facts point in another direction. Sixty-seven percent of the US economy comes from the services industry, and 49.2 percent of people work for small businesses. The biggest opportunity for you is to disrupt the boutique professional services sector.

**Entrepreneurs often don't put innovation and service in the same sentence.**

CHAPTER 6

# THE GO-TO-MARKET

Most CEOs of boutiques are not natural marketers or salespeople. They are experts. Many are giants in their fields. In some cases, some are on TV, the best-seller list, and the speaking circuit. However, when I look at their P&Ls, I am shocked by how little revenue they bring in. How can this be? They would rather go to the dentist than make a sales call. They do not know how to go to market with their services.

**Most CEOs of boutiques are not natural marketers or salespeople.**

Boutiques are for-profit businesses. They have payrolls to meet. This means that they need to be excellent at two things:

1. Attracting new clients
2. Generating additional revenue from existing clients

Marketing and selling services are entirely different from products. Why?

Products are sold and consumed. Services are bought and experienced. Big difference.

For instance, a commercial runs for the latest Lady Gaga song. I buy it on Spotify and listen to it. It was sold to me, I consumed it, and I never met Lady Gaga.

In contrast, if I need an estate plan, I hire an attorney. I find one, we meet, they work with me to produce the estate plan. The service and the person delivering it cannot be separated. The service is experienced, not consumed.

This is a subtle distinction, but it makes all the difference.

A boutique's go-to-market plan must have the following elements:

**Marketing**

- Brand strategy: An inspiring story uniquely relevant to your target clients.
- Value proposition messaging: Explain how a client moves from the problematic status quo to an opportunity-filled future.
- Positioning statements: Articulate why your firm is better than the alternatives.
- Campaign strategy: Hypertargeted efforts that hit the sweet spot of the market.
- Content strategy: Earn brand preference by satisfying the information needs of your target clients.
- Budget: Dollars and nonbillable hours assigned to specific clients to stimulate demand.
- Agency: Trusted service providers who can help execute.
- Lead generation: Attract the right clients to your firm.
- Client marketing: Locate new opportunities inside the

current client base.

**Sales**

- Prospecting process: A consistent way for business developers to find opportunities.
- Buyer journey map: An outline of how a prospective client buys your type of service.
- Sales methodology: A method to convert leads into clients.
- Channel optimization: How the right service will be marketed to the right client at the right time.
- Incentive system: A compensation mechanism that motivates every employee to generate revenue.
- Training: A programmatic approach to increase the effectiveness of each employee when pursuing new opportunities.
- Coverage model: A head-count allocation plan to ensure that the target market is properly covered.

Experts want to help people by solving their problems. The more problems you can solve, the bigger the impact you make. Therefore, reaching clients must happen at scale. This is what a go-to-market plan delivers.

When building your go-to-market plan, consider these questions:

1. Is it obvious to prospects who you serve and how you serve them?

   ☐ yes ☐ no

2. Is it obvious to prospects why you are the best at what you do?

   ☐ yes ☐ no

3. Are you in front of enough prospects to hit your revenue targets?

   ☐ yes ☐ no

4. Do you understand how clients decide to hire someone like you?

   ☐ yes ☐ no

5. Can you consistently win more than 50 percent of the time?

   ☐ yes ☐ no

6. Are you extending your reach through multiple marketing channels?

   ☐ yes ☐ no

7. Are you and your team motivated to bring in revenue?

   ☐ yes ☐ no

8. Are you and your team highly trained to win new business?

   ☐ yes ☐ no

9. Are you covering your market sufficiently?

   ☐ yes ☐ no

10. Do you have an agency capable of multiplying your efforts?

    ☐ yes ☐ no

If you answered yes to eight or more of these questions, you have a well-thought-out, go-to-market plan. The task at hand is to execute it.

If you answered no to eight or more of these questions, your go-to-market engine will not produce enough revenue. The task at hand is to address the gaps.

## SUMMARY

I bet you are an expert in your field. A true giant who knows more about your domain than just about anybody. I am here to tell you that is not enough. If no one knows about your brilliance, what good is it? The world is filled with bankrupt idealists. Master go-to-market. Earn what you deserve. Impact as many people as possible.

CHAPTER 7

# THE ENGAGEMENT

There are two types of business strategies for boutiques. There are firms built around a small number of clients who are each spending a lot. Some refer to these as elephant hunters. They live and die on the big deal. And there are firms built around a large number of clients who are each spending a little. Some refer these to these as rabbit hunters. They live and die on volume. The type of engagement you deliver determines the type of firm you are.

**The type of engagement you deliver determines the type of firm you are.**

Engagements are largely classified by how long they take to complete. In general, the longer they are, the larger they are. For example, I recently met with a management consulting firm. They specialize in strategy development. Their typical engagement was sixty days. This firm spent thirty days in discovery and thirty days in producing a set of recommendations. Their typical engagement cost a client about $100,000.

In contrast, my old firm's typical engagement was nine months.

Our average engagement cost clients about $500,000. The difference was in the type of engagement we performed. We performed discovery and produced recommendations, yes. However, we converted recommendations into solutions. And we implemented the solutions on behalf of the client. This added about seven months to each engagement.

The type of engagement you sell and deliver has many implications. It determines who you market to. It determines how you charge and how you staff. It impacts the number of clients you can serve. The list goes on and on. Therefore, it is essential that you know exactly the type of engagements you deliver.

Here are the yes/no questions to help you think through it:

1. Do you want to serve a small number of clients?

   ☐ yes ☐ no
2. Do you want to live and die on the big deal?

   ☐ yes ☐ no
3. Can you handle the lumpiness that comes with elephant hunting?

   ☐ yes ☐ no
4. Do you want to stay engaged with clients for an extended time period?

   ☐ yes ☐ no
5. Can you get in front of big companies that can afford very large projects?

   ☐ yes ☐ no
6. Can you hire the expensive talent needed to deliver expensive projects?

   ☐ yes ☐ no

7. Can your cash flow support periods of time with low utilization rates?

   ☐ yes ☐ no

8. Is the problem you solve complex enough to warrant long engagements?

   ☐ yes ☐ no

9. Is the service you offer robust enough to require expensive engagements?

   ☐ yes ☐ no

10. Are you comfortable with the risk that comes from high revenue concentration?

    ☐ yes ☐ no

If you answered yes to eight or more of these questions, you are an elephant hunter. The task at hand is to sell and deliver a small number of large deals each year.

If you answered no to eight or more of these questions, you are a rabbit hunter. The task at hand is to sell and deliver a large volume of small deals each year.

## SUMMARY

The type of engagements you sell and deliver determines a lot. The boutiques that offer both types of engagements have a high failure rate. The reason is that matching revenue and expenses with both is very hard. Pick one and be the best you can on that type of engagement.

# CHAPTER 8
# THE MARKET

The size of the prize needs to be worth the effort. Starting a boutique is very rewarding, but it is very difficult. A market with one thousand clients spending $1,000 is worth $1 million. And that assumes you capture 100 percent of it. Not worth it. It takes as much effort to pursue a small market as it does a big market. Therefore, as they say, "Go big or go home."

**It takes as much effort to pursue a small market as it does a big market.**

The size of the addressable market is easy math. It can be oversimplified as the following:

# of clients x $/per engagement = addressable market

For instance, 10,000 possible clients x $10,000 typical engagement = $100 million market.

The bottoms-up question is: "What is my penetration rate going to be?"

Jumping off this example reveals the following:

- One percent penetration = $1 million.

- Five percent penetration = \$5 million
- Ten percent penetration = \$10 million.

As you can see, the levers to pull are engagement size and number of clients. Most client markets will have thousands of potential clients to pursue. Therefore, increasing the number of targets is not helpful. However, increasing the penetration rate is. And increasing the average engagement size is as well.

For example, continuing with the previous example:

5% penetration x \$100,000 per engagement =
500 clients x \$100,000 = \$50 million market

A boutique with \$50 million in revenue will have approximately \$25 million in EBITDA (earnings before interest, taxes, depreciation, and amortization). Assuming an EBITDA multiple of eight times says this boutique is worth \$400 million. Creating \$400 million in wealth is worth it.

I made a mistake along the way that I would like to help you avoid. I did not think through the ability to reach the target market.

For example, there are roughly 12.5 million business-to-business (B2B) companies in the world. My boutique served the B2B head of sales. In our minds, our market size was 12.5 million, as each company had one sales leader. Yet we were wrong for several reasons. Our services were being bought by two people, not one person. The chief marketing officer hired us frequently. This meant that our total market was 25 million, not 12.5 million. In addition, many of these targets were impossible to reach. Their gatekeepers had gatekeepers. This reduced our target market to the early-adopter community. Early adopters for us meant those willing to apply the science of benchmarking to the art of sales. We began publishing content and allowing the early adopters to self-identify by subscribing to it. This started with a book, followed by a blog, podcast, online video, and print magazine. This resulted in a subscriber base of about 250,000 self-identified early adopters. Our average engagement size in those early days was approximately $100,000. Therefore, our available market was $25 billion. One percent penetration was worth $250 million, 5 percent was worth $1.25 billion, and 10 percent was worth $2.5 billion. The size of the prize was worth it, so we went for it. The key lesson is to add the ability to reach the targets to the market-sizing exercise. Big markets that are unreachable are not attractive.

Is your market big enough?

Here are the yes/no questions to think this through:

1. Are there thousands of targets to pursue?

   ☐ yes ☐ no

2. Are they reachable?

   ☐ yes ☐ no

3. When they are reached, will they consider you?

   ☐ yes ☐ no

4. Can you win your fair share of the opportunities?

   ☐ yes ☐ no

5. Can you win your fair share consistently?

   ☐ yes ☐ no

6. When you do win, is the amount of money spent worth the pursuit?

   ☐ yes ☐ no

7. Is the market large enough to support your boutique, assuming modest penetration rates?

   ☐ yes ☐ no

8. Are there new targets to pursue each year—that is, is the market growing?

   ☐ yes ☐ no

9. Can you drive up the engagement size over time?

   ☐ yes ☐ no

10. Will there be a reasonable rate of repeat purchases?

   ☐ yes ☐ no

If you answered yes to eight or more of these questions, your market is attractive. The task at hand is to enter the market and begin competing.

If you answered no to eight or more of these questions, your market is not attractive. The task at hand is to find a market that is more attractive.

## SUMMARY

Pursuing tiny niche markets is a recipe for frustration. Many who start boutiques make this mistake. No one dreams one day of being the best of a bad bunch. Be sure that the size of the prize is worth the amount of effort you put in.

CHAPTER 9

# THE TEAM

Boutiques are best started by teams. It is a myth that great firms are started by a single brilliant person. The ideal team size is three. One person who is great at bringing in clients. One person who is great at servicing the clients. And one person who is great at developing service offerings. At launch, you do not need the overhead functions (HR, IT, legal, finance, etc.). You can outsource all that.

**It is a myth that great firms are started by a single brilliant person.**

There should be very little skills overlap. The idea is that 1 + 1 + 1 = 10. In the beginning, resources are constrained. You cannot afford to be suboptimized with redundant skills.

A friend of mine is a leading provider of jury consulting services. He is a social scientist and helps his clients with jury selection. A few years ago, he and four of his colleagues started their own boutique. They closed shop before their third anniversary. I asked him what happened. It turned out that all five of them enjoyed doing the work. They were driven by the technical aspects of the job. In this case, they loved trial strategy, pretrial research, and witness preparation. However, none of them enjoyed marketing and selling the services. After the initial referral stream dried up, there was not enough work to survive.

This is not uncommon. This team should have been better constructed. It would have been wise to have a great rainmaker as a founding member.

Over time, the biggest department will be the service team. Therefore, this founding partner should be capable of managing a large organization. The service offering development department will stay small. The founder partner here should be an excellent individual contributor. The marketing and sales team will be made up of rainmakers. They will be few, relatively speaking. But they are a pain in the butt. The founding partner here should be a master of managing egos.

Lastly, democracies do not work well in boutiques. Equal partners voting on decisions is too slow. A boutique's advantage is speed. Pick a boss and get in line behind them. Usually the founding partner/rainmaker is the firm's first CEO. The reason is that they are in front of clients pitching work. Clients love speaking to the CEO.

Do you have the right founding team?

Consider these questions:

1. Does your founding team consist of three or more partners?

   ☐ yes ☐ no

2. Is there no overlap in skills among the founding partners?

   ☐ yes ☐ no

3. Is there a loss in capacity due to confusion over who is doing what?

   ☐ yes ☐ no

4. Do you have a partner responsible for acquiring clients?

   ☐ yes ☐ no

5. Do you have a partner responsible for servicing clients?

   ☐ yes ☐ no

6. Do you have a partner responsible for developing service lines?

   ☐ yes ☐ no

7. Can the partner who owns the service department scale to dozens of employees?

   ☐ yes ☐ no

8. Can the partner who owns the marketing and sales department handle big egos?

   ☐ yes ☐ no

9. Is the partner who owns service development comfortable being a lone wolf?

   ☐ yes ☐ no

10. Do the partners complement, rather than compete, with one another?

    ☐ yes ☐ no

If you answered yes to eight or more of these questions, you have a good founding team.

If you answered no to eight or more of these questions, hold off on the launch. Plug the gaps first.

## SUMMARY

It takes a team to realize the dream. The composition of the founding team must be carefully considered. Do not go into business with your friends because they are your friends. Pick your business partners as carefully as you selected your spouse.

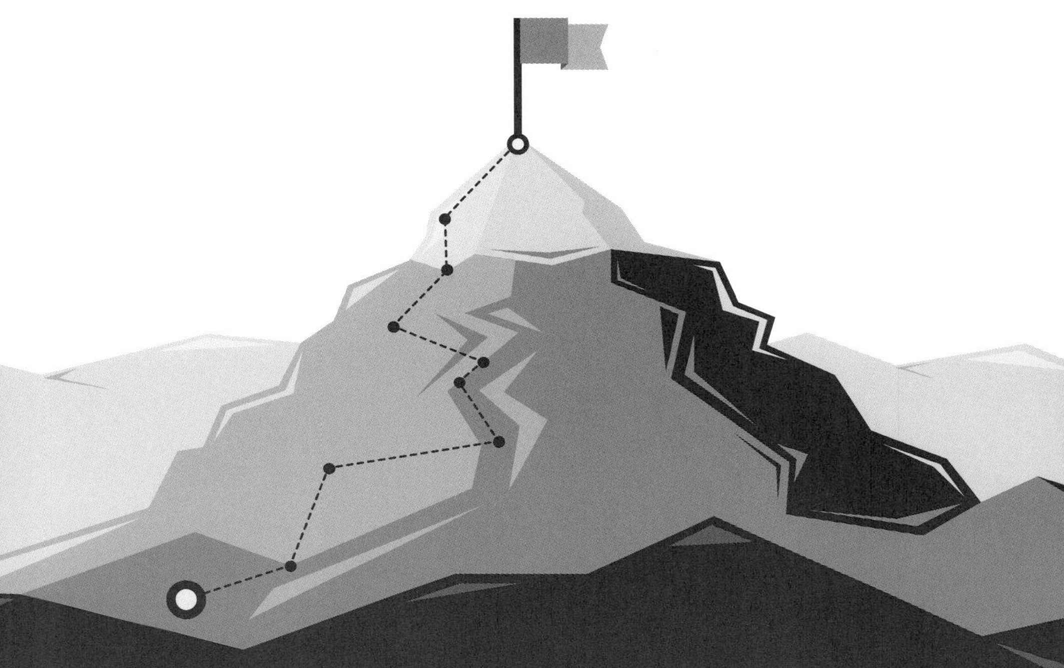

SECTION 2

# SCALE

## CHAPTER 10

# SCALE CAPITAL

Scaling a boutique requires scale capital. Adding more head count, entering new markets, launching new service lines, and other initiatives require money. There are three ways to raise scale capital:

1. Free cash flow from operations.
2. Take debt on the balance sheet.
3. Take on an equity partner.

Free cash flow from operations is the best source of scale capital for boutique owners. It is cheap and in unlimited supply for well-run boutiques. It comes from revenue growth, efficiency improvements, and cost reductions. Scaling with free cash flow preserves the owner's equity. It does not add a debt service burden to the P&L. The best boutiques scale by allocating free cash flow intelligently. However, a reliance on it might result in a boutique taking too long to scale. And human nature

**Free cash flow from operations is the best source of scale capital for boutique owners.**

being what it is, boutique leaders often pay themselves first. Instead of investing in scale, owners pull the extra cash out of the business.

My firm, SBI, used free cash flow from operations as its source of scale capital. In retrospect, this was a mistake. It took me eleven years to start, scale, and sell my boutique. If I had taken on some debt, I could have cut this time in half. We were able to deploy the capital effectively. Each investment resulted in more clients. And each initiative resulted in lower costs. More capital would have resulted in even more clients and lower costs. The cost of the debt capital was much lower than the return we were generating. I was unwilling to take on an equity partner. I did not want to dilute my stake. This, as it turned out, was the right decision. However, I should have borrowed. Why did I not take on the debt? I did not recognize the opportunity cost at the time. As a young man in my thirties, I felt that I had decades to reach the goal. This was foolish, as tomorrow is never guaranteed. A lot can go wrong in a decade.

Balance sheet debt is the next best source of scale capital for boutique owners. It is not cheap, but it is reasonable, as lenders charge modest rates on loans to boutiques. There is less supply, as lenders typically cap loans at two to three times EBITDA. It comes from banks or private lenders. It does add a debt service expense to the P&L. This will reduce the boutique owner's income. But it does preserve owner equity. Young boutiques often cannot get it unless they personally guarantee the loan. And in some cases, a personal guarantee does not work. The owner's personal assets are insufficient.

An equity partner is an investor that buys into the boutique. It is cheap in the short run but expensive in the long run. There is no debt service hit to the P&L protecting the owner's income. However, the owner's stake is diluted, as the equity investor owns a piece of the firm. They are entitled to ownership distributions. And when you sell the firm, the equity investor takes their share of the pie. Traditionally, equity investors do not invest in boutiques due to the perceived high risk. This makes it difficult for boutiques to raise scale capital from this source. It is in short supply.

Which is the best source of scale capital for you?

Here are the yes/no questions to help you answer this:

1. Are you generating enough free cash flow to fund scale?

   ☐ yes ☐ no
2. Do you know where to deploy this extra free cash flow?

   ☐ yes ☐ no
3. Are you willing to go without today for scale tomorrow?

   ☐ yes ☐ no
4. Have you been in business for at least five years?

   ☐ yes ☐ no
5. Are you generating stable EBITDA every year?

   ☐ yes ☐ no
6. Would two to three times EBITDA be enough to fund your scale?

   ☐ yes ☐ no
7. Can your P&L handle the debt service burden of a loan?

   ☐ yes ☐ no
8. Are you willing to personally guarantee a loan?

   ☐ yes ☐ no
9. Do you have enough personal assets to secure the loan if open to a guarantee?

   ☐ yes ☐ no
10. Are you willing to dilute your ownership stake for the right equity partner?

    ☐ yes ☐ no

If you answered yes to eight or more of these questions, all three sources of scale capital are available to you. The task at hand is to choose the right one for you.

If you answered to no to questions 1 through 3, do not pursue free cash flow. The task at hand is to consider debt or equity.

If you answered no to questions 4 through 9, do not pursue debt. The task at hand is to consider improving free cash flow or selling equity.

If you answered no to question 10, do not pursue an equity partner. The task at hand is to improve free cash flow or to raise debt.

## SUMMARY

Scaling a boutique takes money. This type of money is called scale capital. There are three primary sources of scale capital. Each has a set of advantages and disadvantages. Which is best for you is highly situational. All work well when applied correctly. If raising scale capital makes you uncomfortable, do not attempt to scale. Many people are happy with lifestyle businesses.

## CHAPTER 11

# LEVERAGE

Boutiques trying to scale need to figure out how to increase their leverage ratio. A leverage ratio is the number of nonpartners to partners. For instance, a firm that has thirty employees and three partners/owners has a ratio of 10:1. Why is this important? If partners/owners must be everywhere and do everything, they become a bottleneck. If they can leverage themselves, they can scale the boutique.

**The type of work the boutique performs determines the type of employees they hire.**

The type of work the boutique performs determines the type of employees they hire. And the type of employees a boutique hires determines its leverage ratio. For instance, if the engagements require a high skill level, the leverage ratio will be small. It is impossible to proceduralize this work, which means that juniors cannot do it. In contrast, if the work is routine, junior employees can handle it. In this instance, leverage will be high.

An owner of a boutique custom software development shop

came to see me. He could not understand why he was working harder and making less. He had plenty of business but just could not figure out how to scale. I asked him what type of projects he took on. He spoke for an hour before he came up for air. It turned out that every engagement was a one-off. This made it impossible for him to staff his firm correctly. He never knew what type of skills he would need. He and a few of his superstars pretty much did all the work. After a couple of years filled with seventy-hour weeks, they were burned out. They had no leverage. They were running in place.

Are you suffering from poor leverage?

Run yourself through these yes/no questions to find out:

1. Is your leverage of employee to owner at least 10:1?

   ☐ yes ☐ no

2. Is the proper mix of low, middle, and senior staff clear to you?

   ☐ yes ☐ no

3. Do you understand the skills mix required for an engagement before you sign it?

   ☐ yes ☐ no

4. Do you understand which revenue is "good" and which is "bad"?

   ☐ yes ☐ no

5. Do you have a zero-tolerance policy for one-off projects?

   ☐ yes ☐ no

6. Do the partners/owners work on the business instead of in the business?

   ☐ yes ☐ no

7. Do your service offerings come with procedure manuals

for the delivery staff?

☐ yes ☐ no

8. Do you assign work to project teams strategically versus reactionally?

☐ yes ☐ no

9. Does your hiring plan forecast demand for a specific leverage ratio?

☐ yes ☐ no

10. Do your financial goals match up with the leverage ratio assumptions in your business plan?

☐ yes ☐ no

If you answered yes to eight or more of these questions, leverage is not preventing you from scale. The task at hand is to turn your attention to other areas.

If you answered no to eight or more of these questions, poor leverage might be preventing scale. The task at hand is to adjust your model.

## SUMMARY

Boutique firms often grow but do not scale. Growth means more projects delivered with the same type of staff. If nothing changes, then the growth rate is proportional to the number of partners/owners required. This means that the profit pool increases, but it must be shared with more partners/owners. More growth means the need for more partners/owners. This results in a bigger boutique but no increase in income or wealth for the founders. Improved leverage means improved incomes and wealth for the founders.

## CHAPTER 12

# CASH FLOW

Cash flow is to a boutique what oxygen is to a human. If there is not enough of it, both die. Cash flow simply means the money coming in and going out of the boutique. It is different from net income. Cash flow comes from daily operating activities. Net income is the profit a boutique makes for a period. It is often calculated annually for tax purposes. Cash flow is also different from EBITDA. For instance, EBITDA does not consider capital expenditures, which are cash outflows.

> **Cash flow is to a boutique what oxygen is to a human.**

The two most effective ways to look at cash flow are as follows:

1. Cash flow per partner
2. Cash flow per project

The team at Capital 54 recently performed due diligence on a public relations firm. They used the following formula:

Cash flow/partner = cash flow/fees x fees/staff x staff/partners

This revealed a healthy $650,000 in cash flow per partner. This told us that there was enough free cash flow being generated from operations. The business plan called for aggressive expansion, and the funds were available. This boutique was poised to scale.

In contrast, this same team recently looked at a commercial photography boutique. The unit of measure was cash flow per project. The variables here were fee, number of hours per staff member, fully loaded cost per staff member, and allocated overhead. This revealed too much cash flow volatility for us, and we passed. Some projects produced a lot of cash flow and others produced negative cash flow. The implication was that the delivery model was not standardized and therefore not scalable.

Are you wondering if your cash flow is enough to scale your boutique?

This chapter's yes/no questions should be helpful:

1. Will you run out of working capital if you double your firm?

   ☐ yes ☐ no

2. Will you need a lot of short-term debt if you double your firm?

   ☐ yes ☐ no

3. Will you develop a collections problem if you double your firm?

   ☐ yes ☐ no

4. Will your cash payments exceed your cash income if you double your firm?

   ☐ yes ☐ no

5. Will you have a hard time getting enough cash on the balance sheet to double your firm?

   ☐ yes ☐ no

6. When growth has spiked in the past, did your cash flow ever turn negative?

   ☐ yes ☐ no

7. Will payroll growth exceed accounts receivable growth when you double your boutique?

   ☐ yes ☐ no

8. Will cash flow problems be hidden due to lack of forward visibility?

   ☐ yes ☐ no

9. Will it be hard to generate yield on your cash deposits?

   ☐ yes ☐ no

10. Will you be at risk of paying your future obligations if you double your firm?

    ☐ yes ☐ no

If you answered no to eight or more of these questions, cash flow will not be an obstacle to scale. The task at hand is to focus elsewhere.

If you answered yes to eight or more of these questions, cash flow will prevent scale. The task at hand is to improve the management of your cash flow.

## SUMMARY

Boutiques run on cash. They do not run on net income or EBITDA. Some boutiques neglect the management of cash flow. Take a moment to understand how you can improve the flow in and out.

CHAPTER 13

# LIFE CYCLE

Boutiques, like people, have a life cycle. And some boutiques have multiple life cycles. For example, the firm has its life cycle, and the service lines have life cycles. Locating where your boutique is on the life-cycle curve is important when trying to scale.

The team at Collective 54 has determined that there are three types of boutiques:

1. Intellect: Clients hire these boutiques to solve difficult, one-of-a-kind problems.
2. Wisdom: Clients hire these boutiques because they have been there and done that.
3. Method: Clients hire these boutiques because of their unique methodologies.

At times, boutiques suffer from an identity crisis. They are unsure of the type of firm they are. They are unsure of the type of clients and engagements they should pursue. This makes the challenge of managing a boutique harder than it needs to be. Conflicting client needs drive confusing staffing models, which lead to complex financials. One month there is not enough to do. The next month the firm is 120 percent of capacity. This prevents scale.

I was advising a geology firm in Houston in 2019. The founder's grandson recently took over from his dad. As is typical, this young guy wanted to make a name for himself. He was going to scale this sixty-year-old lifestyle business. He began hiring young talent with modern skills, and together they went after a new type of client. Before long, he had an eclectic mix of clients. Some had been with the firm for decades. They wanted the "old-school" services. Some followed the new talent to his firm. These clients wanted the work done the way the previous firm did it. And some clients were brand new. They wanted the new "tech-enabled" services.

Each of these clients was at different stage of the life cycle. Young, old, new, small, medium, large, and one mega client. The young man was making a lot of enemies. Sacred cows were no longer sacred. Glass was getting broken, and yet there was no scale. It is practically impossible to scale a boutique this way.

He eventually placed each client into one of the three categories: intellect, wisdom, and method. He categorized his service offerings into the same buckets. He analyzed how an intellect client moved to a wisdom client. And how a wisdom client moved to a method client. He recognized that today's pioneering approach is tomorrow's commodity. And he became aware that this is happening faster today than before. The young gun reorganized around a divisional organizational structure with separate P&L statements. A general manager was hired to run the three separate divisions. Clients' needs were mapped to employee skills, which were mapped to service line life cycles.

And the firm is scaling.

Are you wondering what type of firm you are? Or where you are on the life cycle?

Consider these questions:

1. Do your clients hire you for never-before-seen problems?

   ☐ yes ☐ no

2. Do you employ leading experts in the field?

   ☐ yes ☐ no

3. Do you have legally protected intellectual property?

   ☐ yes ☐ no

If you answered yes to these questions, you are an intellect firm.

4. Do your clients hire you because you have solved their problem before?

   ☐ yes ☐ no

5. Do your clients hire you because you have direct, relevant case studies?

   ☐ yes ☐ no

6. Do your clients hire you because you help them avoid common mistakes?

   ☐ yes ☐ no

If you answered yes to these questions, you are a wisdom firm.

7. Do your clients hire you because they are busy and need an extra pair of hands?

   ☐ yes ☐ no

8. Do your clients hire you because you can get the work done quickly?

   ☐ yes ☐ no

9. Do your clients hire you because you have an army of trained people to deploy immediately?

   ☐ yes ☐ no

If you answered yes to these questions, you are a method firm.

10. Do your service offerings start out as leading edge and over time become commodities?

   ☐ yes ☐ no

If you answered yes to this question, you need to master life-cycle management. If not, this will prevent scale.

## SUMMARY

**Boutiques with poor cash flow and low client satisfaction do not scale.**

A lack of life-cycle awareness and management prevents scale. It results in expensive senior people doing junior work. This destroys cash flow. And it results in inexperienced junior people doing senior work. This destroys client satisfaction. Boutiques with poor cash flow and low client satisfaction do not scale.

CHAPTER 14

# YIELD

The yield of a boutique is the measure of productivity. Yield is simply the average fee per hour times the average utilization rate of the team. For instance, if the boutique's average fee per hour is $400 and the average utilization rate is 75 percent, then the yield is $300 per hour.

The typical boutique runs off an assumption of a forty-hour week and forty-eight weeks per year. This equates to 1,920 hours per employee. At $300 per hour, the firm will do $576,000 per employee. Therefore, a one-hundred-person firm will have an annual revenue of $57.6 million.

Most boutiques can quote you their utilization rate from memory. This is a well-tracked metric, as it should be. Boutiques that have made it past the start-up stage have already optimized for their utilization rate. They would not have survived otherwise. Therefore, an improvement in utilization rate does not lead to scale. The point of diminishing returns has occurred. Unless, of course, you are going to ask employees to work on Christmas Day.

To scale, owners of boutiques need to turn to fees. This is not as simple as raising prices. Most boutiques are in competitive markets.

The intense competition drives downward pressure on fees. Instead, boutiques must become more valuable to their clients. Clients will pay more for boutiques that bring more value to them.

**Clients will pay more for boutiques that bring more value to them.**

Clients turn to boutiques for specialization. These clients have moved away from generalists. They are willing to pay more for specialists. Here are the forms of specialization that drive up yield:

- Industry
- Function
- Segment
- Problem
- Geography

A hypothetical example would be a consulting firm that helps product managers at enterprise software companies in Silicon Valley move to the cloud.

If this firm were to exist, it would be perceived by clients to be highly specialized. Notice the industry: software companies. The function: product managers. The segment: enterprise. The problem: move to the cloud. The geography: Silicon Valley.

This firm's yield will be high because they can charge more.

Screen yourself for yield against these questions:

1. Are your average utilization rates above 85 percent?

   ☐ yes ☐ no

2. Senior staff above 70 percent?

   ☐ yes ☐ no

3. Midlevel staff above 80 percent?

   ☐ yes ☐ no

4. Junior staff above 90 percent?

   ☐ yes ☐ no

5. Are your average fees above $400?

   ☐ yes ☐ no

6. Senior staff above $750?

   ☐ yes ☐ no

7. Midlevel staff above $500?

   ☐ yes ☐ no

8. Junior staff above $250?

   ☐ yes ☐ no

9. Are you assuming at least forty-eight weeks and forty hours per week?

   ☐ yes ☐ no

10. Are you distinguished from the generalist with three to five forms of specialization?

    ☐ yes ☐ no

If you answered yes to eight or more of these questions, you are running a tight ship. Yield is not your obstacle to scale. Focus elsewhere.

If you answered no to eight or more of these questions, yield is an issue. You need to get your house in order. Do so before trying to scale.

## SUMMARY

Yield is the most looked-at metric for boutiques. Owners and CEOs obsess over utilization rates. Many have reached the point of diminishing returns. More attention needs to be placed on making your boutique more valuable to clients. There are many ways to do that. However, hyperspecialization has the highest probability of success.

CHAPTER 15

# PRICING

A change to your pricing strategy is, perhaps, the quickest way to scale. Why? It is does not require an investment in people or money to implement. And the benefits are immediate: charge more today than you did yesterday.

Most boutiques price their services incorrectly for these reasons:

- Boutiques do not know what their services are worth to their clients.
- Boutiques do not know what their clients are willing to pay.
- Boutiques cannot logically explain to clients why they charge what they charge.
- Boutiques cannot quantify the amount of value a client receives from an engagement.
- The pricing approach is inward out—that is, based on internal costs.
- Boutiques rely too heavily on what their competitors charge for similar services.

- Sales teams inside boutiques cannot overcome pricing objectives effectively.

The good news is that this problem is simply solved. It takes some sound judgment, but pricing best practices are readily available. Here are a few to get you started.

**Connect your pricing strategy to your business strategy.**

Develop a pricing strategy that matches your business strategy. For example, if you sell to small businesses, the high-volume, low-price model makes sense. If you sell luxury items to the elite, the low-volume, high-cost approach is best. If you sell differentiated products to midtier customers, premium pricing makes sense. For instance, a Lexus costs more than a Camry but less than a Rolls-Royce. Connect your pricing strategy to your business strategy.

Perception is reality in pricing. Therefore, price positioning is very important. The price you charge sends a signal to the client. The price influences how a client perceives you. If you price too low, your work will be considered low quality. If you price too high, you will be perceived as being difficult to engage. If you price the same as your competitors, you will be perceived as a commodity. Clients value specific attributes of your service offering. Understand what those are and influence the perception of your performance in these areas.

An example from my past might help you appreciate the power of perception. The structure of the management consulting industry has three tiers. The first tier is the large market leaders. The second tier is the midsize boutiques. The third tier is the small start-ups or one-man shops. My firm, SBI, was a tier-two management consulting firm. A midsize boutique. We priced our services below the first tier but above the second tier. What perception did this send to clients?

It said that we were the best of the boutiques. Clients who wanted to hire a boutique but were afraid to hired us. These clients felt that moving away from a brand-name firm was risky. Yet they were willing to take the chance because hiring us reduced the risk. We were the best of the boutiques and close to the tier-one providers. The perception the price set was that my firm was a premium boutique. This was a powerful differentiator.

Use price versioning to allow clients to choose their own price. This will result in them deciding on a proposal faster. Giving clients a choice allows the boutique to link price and value. Price is what you pay. Value is what you get. And the two are never the same. For example, personal trainers sell packages to their clients. The bronze package is $/visit. The silver package is $/fitness program. The gold package is $/wellness program. The choice allows the client to think about what they value: visits, fitness programs, or a wellness program.

Are you wondering whether a new pricing strategy would help you scale?

Answer these questions to find out:

1. Do you know what your offering is worth to clients?

   ☐ yes ☐ no

2. Can you quantify the value of your work in hard dollars?

   ☐ yes ☐ no

3. Do you know what clients are willing to pay for your services?

   ☐ yes ☐ no

4. Can you explain the logic of your pricing in a way that makes sense to clients?

   ☐ yes ☐ no

5. Does your price illustrate to the client the link between price and value?

   ☐ yes ☐ no

6. Do you charge the most for the service features that your clients want the most?

   ☐ yes ☐ no

7. Do you charge the least for the service features that your clients don't care much about?

   ☐ yes ☐ no

8. Do you allow your clients to choose their price by presenting options?

   ☐ yes ☐ no

9. Is your sales team skilled at overcoming price objections?

   ☐ yes ☐ no

10. Have you built into your system an annual price increase?

    ☐ yes ☐ no

If you answered yes to eight or more of these questions, pricing is not your problem. Keep doing what you are doing.

If you answered no to eight or more of these questions, pricing is an issue. It makes sense for you to consider developing a new pricing strategy.

## SUMMARY

Know your worth. Don't undervalue yourself. What you do is exceptional. Price accordingly. The clients you want know this and will pay you with a smile. You do not want the clients who are unwilling to pay you fairly.

# CHAPTER 16
# REPLICATION

Leaders of boutiques have a hard time replicating themselves in their employees. They are control freaks. They would rather do something themselves than delegate it. They believe that the time it takes to teach, and delegate, is not worth it. It is just faster to do "it" themselves. If they do it, it will be done correctly. This attitude prevents scale. If not addressed, the boutique becomes a stagnant lifestyle business.

Why?

Profits take a big hit as a result of underdelegation. It results in expensive senior people doing work that inexpensive junior people could do. Employee development is retarded with this approach. Junior staff need to learn on the job. If the leaders of boutiques do everything, the staff will not grow. This destroys morale and leads to high turnover. If a boutique is turning over employees, it cannot scale.

**If a boutique is turning over employees, it cannot scale.**

The primary reason this happens is that boutiques report

on profitability incorrectly. The unit of measure of profit for a healthy boutique is the project. Boutiques' financial performance is the sum of their projects. When owners perform work that can be delegated, project profitability goes down. Owners are expensive labor. Engagement managers should be looking to increase leverage in every project. They should be held accountable for project profitability. If they were, the replication problem would go away. Cost to deliver would be considered as much as utilization rates. What gets measured gets managed.

On a single project, it will always be less efficient to deploy junior staff. You will have to supervise their work. They will take longer to complete tasks. However, in the long run, well-trained junior staff solve the replication problem. Owners do not have to do everything. They do not have to be everywhere. The firm becomes independent of the owner(s). It can grow, and scale, without them. This is the objective, especially if you want to sell someday.

The solution to this problem is employee certification. Employee certification is a process to prove that an employee has achieved a level of competency. If done correctly, this can rapidly scale a boutique.

In professional services there are two capabilities to certify:

1. Knowledge
2. Skills

Knowledge is the practical understanding of your domain. For example, an accounting firm needs to understand GAAP, or generally accepted accounting principles. Boutiques are hired by clients because they are experts in an area. If you are the expert, clients will require you to be involved in every project. This does not scale. Your expertise must be replicated in your staff. You need many experts in your firm. And growing your own is more profitable than seeking hired guns.

Skills are the ability to do something. For instance, consultants often must interview executives. Conducting an effective interview is a skill. There is a proper way to open, ask questions, follow up, and close. If employees lack skills, owners of boutiques must do everything themselves. This does not scale.

Building a certification program is straightforward. It begins with postmortems of recent engagements. The engagements should be a representative sample of what you do. Break down each project. Seek to understand the exact knowledge required for each engagement. Look at how the work was performed at the task level. Inventory the skills requirements to perform each task.

The knowledge and skills requirements should be converted into an exam. The exam should consist of questions to test an employee. The answers should categorize an employee. I prefer the 101, 201, and 301 model used in academia. Under 101 results in termination—too big of an upskilling effort: 101 says you are junior, 201 says you are midlevel, and 301 says you are expert.

Administer the test. This will baseline your employee base. You will understand the capability of your team. The tests results populate an employee database. The database is used in two ways. First, it is relied on when staffing engagements. As work comes in, you assign projects to teams based on their ability. Second, it triggers the employee learning management system. Each employee is placed into a learning path. At the end of the path are fully trained 301 employees. And when each employee is 301 certified, the replication problem is solved.

The time-consuming piece is creating the learning content. The owner(s) must get out of their head what they know. It needs to be converted into learning content. And it needs to be maintained. The best way to do this is to rent an instructional designer. I recommend someone who understands adult learning. This professional will save you a lot of time and money. They will extract your tribal knowledge and convert it into courseware. This courseware will be organized into a learning management system. Employees can consume it on their mobile devices. You can monitor progress and track to a set of goals.

Are you suffering from poor replication?

Ask yourself these questions to find out:

1. Do you feel like you must do everything yourself?

   ☐ yes ☐ no

2. Do you feel like you must be in every key meeting?

   ☐ yes ☐ no

3. Do clients require you to be directly involved in their projects?

   ☐ yes ☐ no

4. Do your employees come to you for help constantly?

   ☐ yes ☐ no

5. Do you have to micromanage everyone?

   ☐ yes ☐ no

6. Do you have to review everything before it goes out?

   ☐ yes ☐ no

7. Are you working too much?

   ☐ yes ☐ no

8. Is it faster to just do the work yourself?

   ☐ yes ☐ no

9. Do you feel like it will get done correctly only if you do it?

   ☐ yes ☐ no

10. Are you turning over employees?

    ☐ yes ☐ no

If you answered yes to eight or more of these questions, you have a replication problem. The task is to implement knowledge and skills certification.

If you answered no to eight or more of these questions, you do not have a replication problem. Good for you.

## SUMMARY

Boutique owners suffer from the hero syndrome. They have their personal identity wrapped up in their firms. When they are needed, it feels good. It validates them. This insecurity gets in the way of scaling the firm. The best owners work themselves out of a job. They make themselves obsolete. The firm can succeed without them. This is when hyperscale kicks in.

CHAPTER 17

# CULTURE

Nearly all boutique owners feel that culture is an important part of their success. However, few understand how to scale their culture. This failure causes the culture to erode as the boutique gets larger and older. What was once a strength of the firm becomes a weakness.

Culture can be simply explained as how things get done at your boutique. Defining the way your boutique does things matters. Scaling requires focused action. Hazy cultures get in the way of scaling. As you add employees, they need know how to behave. Unclear cultures create confusion, which turns into politics.

Ask a random sample of your employees these questions:

- What are the firm's goals?
- How are you personally trying to help the firm achieve these goals?
- When you must make trade-offs, which of the firm's values are prioritized?
- What kind of behavior do you hire for?
- Which types of behaviors do you promote?

- Which types of behaviors get people fired?

In the start-up phase, you get the same answers to these questions from all employees. When you scale, you get different answers from the employees. The culture starts to erode.

Culture is particularly critical during the scaling phase. Scaling can be messy. The chaotic nature of scaling means that employees work while the rules start to break down. As previous directives are replaced with new procedures, employees struggle with fear. They need to know how to behave, and a strong culture helps.

Most successful boutiques that scale are known for their distinctive cultures. Typically, the credit goes to you, the founder/owner. The personality of the founder/owner plays a critical role in culture formation. However, the boutique's culture emerges over time based on the actions of many people.

**Most successful boutiques that scale are known for their distinctive cultures.**

The dominant culture typically originates inside the most important function. For example, my firm was a sales consultancy. We hired sales experts in the B2B field. As a result, it was the sales function at SBI that set the tone. Ours was a competitive culture where one was only as good as their last win. However, there are many different types of cultures. For instance, some boutiques are engineering driven, product focused, client obsessed, design centered, marketing based, finance or ops concentrated. All these cultures can be successful. The important lesson for your boutique to scale is to focus on the mission-critical function. And the leader of that function should be the leader of the boutique's culture.

The scaling of a culture is important in branding. Culture is the story you tell yourself, your employees, and your clients. It describes who you are and your place in the world. And it is the story others will tell about you.

The best way to scale a culture is a mix of nature and nurture. Nature, in this sense, is to let the culture scale organically. Nurture, in this sense, is trying to define the culture as part of strategy. Too much nature, and the risk is great; the culture will erode as you scale. Too much nurture, and the culture will become rigid and inflexible.

In scaling boutiques, maintaining culture becomes increasingly difficult. In the start-up stage, early employees feel bonded to one another. In the scaling stage, more employees come onboard. Spontaneous interactions give way to formalized structures. Natural transmission of culture happens through personal interactions. Owners in scaling boutiques no longer have personal interactions with every employee. The person-to-person culture transmission is impossible for scaling boutiques.

During scale, employees need to help recreate the culture. New employees quickly become the old school because a lot of people are joining. It is important that these new old-schoolers remember what they like about your boutique. And they need to make sure that these things last.

Start-up employees fear that with scale comes bureaucracy. And, unfortunately, this does happen in some cases. But it does not need to. A strong culture can be a substitute for bureaucracy and rules. The stronger the owner makes the culture, the less the owner needs to be law enforcement.

Owners who have scaled tell me about two actions they took. First, they overcommunicated. These owners maintained a direct line to employees. There are many ways to do this: town hall meetings, weekly newsletters, contests, and so on.

Allow me to share a personal story as to how I did this. A cultural bedrock at my firm was risk-taking. I wanted every employee to go for it. The quickest way to get fired at SBI was to play it safe. I hired high-growth people trapped in low-growth environments. When they joined my firm, they were liberated. Big companies strangled them, but I unleashed their potential. To encourage risk-taking, I held periodic fuckup contests. Employees would present their biggest fuckups on a firm-wide teleconference. The employee who shared the best lesson learned from the fuckup was given a $1,000 bonus. This was a public reinforcement of our culture. It was a scale activity, and it was a firm-wide event. The employees who won the prize were the ones who swung for the fences. And we celebrated them. Fuckups were heroes.

In addition to overcommunicating, scaling culture changes employee management practices. Who you hire, promote, and fire determines how a culture scales. The people you hire determine your culture. Yet scaling boutiques require lots of bodies, so they get lazy in their hiring. For example, they often overpay so-called A players. This results in a boutique filled with hit men, people who work for the money only. And if you are growing 30 to 50 percent per year, in two to three years, all you have is hit men. One day the owner wakes up and the culture is destroyed.

Another common mistake owners make is promoting the wrong people. With scale comes the need for management layers on the organizational chart. These roles are often filled with the wrong people. This results in a culture being driven by inexperienced managers.

All these are reasons to scale your culture as you scale your boutique. Overcommunicating and hiring, promoting, and firing for culture is the path forward. Employees join, stay for a while, and leave. They are replaced by new employees, and the cycle repeats. An owner cannot assume that the culture will perpetuate through this turnover. Proactive culture management is required to scale it. And scaling it is a must if you want to scale.

Here are some questions to determine whether culture is preventing you from scaling:

1. Is your culture important to the success of your boutique?

   ☐ yes ☐ no

2. Does every employee understand the "way things get done around here"?

   ☐ yes ☐ no

3. Does every employee understand what you are trying to accomplish?

   ☐ yes ☐ no

4. Does every employee understand how they personally contribute to these goals?

   ☐ yes ☐ no

5. Is it clear which behaviors are rewarded?

   ☐ yes ☐ no

6. Is it clear which behaviors are punished?

   ☐ yes ☐ no

7. Is it clear which function inside the boutique is the dominant function?

   ☐ yes ☐ no

8. Is the leader of this function the leader of the boutique?

   ☐ yes ☐ no

9. Is the culture scaling naturally the way you want it to?

   ☐ yes ☐ no

10. Are you nurturing the culture as you scale?

    ☐ yes ☐ no

## SUMMARY

Culture allows a boutique to retain its identify as it scales. Culture is a welcome substitute for bureaucracy that can plague scaling boutiques. Get the nature and nurture correct to proactively scale the culture.

## CHAPTER 18

# BUSINESS DEVELOPMENT

As a boutique graduates from start-up to scale, business development needs to change. The primary difference is that scale firms have a client roster. This means that they can generate revenue from existing clients. Start-ups spend their business development efforts exclusively on acquiring new clients. Scale firms split their time between acquiring new clients and developing existing clients. This ignites growth. Why? It is a lot easier to sell to existing clients.

The cost to acquire a new client is expensive. It takes a long time. Start-ups must get in front of the new client. This requires a marketing push and time for word of mouth to spread. Articles get written and published. Speeches at conferences get made. Podcasts get produced and books get written. Social media accounts get filled with posts. The wide net catches a lot of fish that need to be qualified. RFPs require responses.

**The cost to acquire a new client is expensive.**

Competitive bake-offs require decks to be created. Opportunities must be managed with care. Relationships need to be nurtured. Lots of miles get logged and many hotel beds get filled. References need to be contacted. I am exhausted just writing about it. All these activities take a consistent level of effort. This requires staff, time, and budget. It is very expensive.

Scale boutiques do far less of this. Yes, a steady stream of new clients is essential to the health of a boutique. However, scale boutiques get repeat business from existing clients. This revenue reduces the need for new clients. And it costs much less to generate; thus, it spikes profits. If you are interested in guidance on acquiring new clients, see chapter 6. My attention here will be on generating revenue from existing clients. This is the scale activity.

To start, you need a budget. The business development budget should have two items:

1. Dollars
2. Hours

Dollars are the discretionary funds you will use to invest in your existing clients. Hours are the nonbillable time your staff will invest in existing clients. Boutiques often assume, incorrectly, that business from existing clients just happens. This is not true. It requires investment in time and money.

A boutique in the energy efficiency inspection business is an example of excellence. They provide energy audits for companies that are looking for ways to reduce utility bills. The technicians have been cross-trained in the firm's business development process. While delivering the work, they are listening for new opportunities. The technicians' expense reports are heavily monitored. However, the goal is not to reduce expenses but to increase them. The owners want the technicians to make the client feel important. For instance, they often show up at the job with Starbucks for everyone. The clients trust the technicians because they are not salespeople. These technicians often point out needs that the client was unaware of. These leads fill the funnel. In some cases, they convert to billings instantly. The cost to acquire this type of business is very little.

Boutiques are often horrified the first time they do a share of wallet exercise. This reveals how much of a client's total spend is spent with you. Boutiques assume that they are getting 100 percent of a client's business. They are not. Clients have new needs all the time. They give business to other firms without you even knowing about it. Why? They are unaware of your full capabilities. Unless something is seriously wrong with the relationship, this should be yours. Capturing this low-hanging fruit is a simple way to scale.

Which of your clients can give you additional business? How can you invest to capture this business? Which activities are most likely to result in success?

The solution to this problem is easily implemented. Start by doing a share of wallet exercise. This should include current and previous clients. This will produce a list of accounts you should invest in. Focus first on your current client roster. You have a team deployed there right now. Redesign your business development process and prioritize listening for new opportunities. Train your teams on the new process. Task them with identifying new opportunities on these clients. Next, go back to previous clients. Nurture these relationships. Invest nonbillable time in a set of activities that these clients would value. Develop a business development process specific to these clients. Assign a team to them and train them on the new process. Hold them accountable for reactivating these dormant clients.

Boutiques should generate approximately 80 percent of their

revenue from existing clients and 20 percent from new clients. If your numbers differ significantly, rethink your business development efforts.

Still unsure if you should focus on this?

Screen yourself against these questions:

1. Are you generating a lot of business from existing clients?

   ☐ yes ☐ no

2. Have you reduced your need for new clients substantially?

   ☐ yes ☐ no

3. Do you understand your share of wallet for your current clients?

   ☐ yes ☐ no

4. Are your current clients up to date on your full capabilities?

   ☐ yes ☐ no

5. Are you investing nonbillable hours directly into your existing clients?

   ☐ yes ☐ no

6. Have you redesigned your business development process to prioritize existing clients?

   ☐ yes ☐ no

7. Have you trained your employees on the new business development process?

   ☐ yes ☐ no

8. Are your "delivery teams" goaled and measured on finding new opportunities?

   ☐ yes ☐ no

9. Are the employees who are best at business development your cultural heroes?

   ☐ yes ☐ no

10. Do you make sure that your current clients know how important they are to you?

    ☐ yes ☐ no

If you answered yes to eight or more of these questions, you do not have a business development problem. You are well on your way to scaling.

If you answered no to eight or more of these questions, you have a problem. You may still be in start-up mode and overly dependent on new-client acquisition.

## SUMMARY

As you scale, life gets easier. You have happy clients. They buy more from you. They refer their friends to you. You win more business as word of mouth spreads the brand. Your win rate goes up. And your cost to acquire business goes down. Make sure this is happening at your firm.

## CHAPTER 19

# SERVICE OFFERING DEVELOPMENT

As we read in the last chapter, existing client revenue growth is key to scale. This requires having more to offer clients over time. If you keep bringing them the same thing, they will become fatigued. Service offering development becomes a priority as boutiques scale.

Let me share my personal story to make this point. I launched SBI in 2006. I had one service offering. It was called talent management. It was a methodology to interview and hire salespeople. I coauthored a book explaining it, called *Topgrading for Sales*. My target client was the head of sales at large B2B companies. The problem I was going after was clear. The cost of making a single hiring mistake was about $500,000. Many of these companies made dozens of hiring mistakes per year. The problem was costing them millions. This got us in the door.

As my firm got hired and we performed, clients asked us to do more. For example, they needed help designing sales territories. Setting quotas and designing compensation plans were particularly difficult.

And optimizing sales channels was a common request. I had two ways to address these opportunities. First, I could refer the business to business partners. This would have been an easy way to earn quick cash via a referral fee. Or I could develop the capability in-house. This was costly in the short term but lucrative in the long term. I chose to invest the resources to develop the services in-house. Over time, SBI's offerings expanded dramatically. When I left, the firm had more than one hundred service offerings. We launched about ten per year. Eventually, we packaged them into a trademarked offering called the Revenue Growth Methodology. The price I got for the firm was 30 percent above comparable firms. And this was in part due to the robustness of the offering. If we did not develop new offerings, I would be running a little lifestyle business right now.

**To scale, you need to bring new service offerings to market.**

To scale, you need to bring new service offerings to market.

The best way to do this is to listen intently to clients and prospects. They will tell you what they need. I am not referring to the informal listening that happens naturally. And I am not talking about reading secondary market research. I am suggesting direct primary market research. There are several ways that boutiques can do this well.

Start with a simple question: "What do our clients want?" Don't be arrogant and assume that you know. Your opinion does not matter. The only person who can answer this question is the client.

Focus first on the existing clients. Invite a handful to be on your client advisory board. Start with approximately ten clients, half existing clients and half former clients. Get together with them twice a year. Each session should be a day and a half. Send out prework and make sure that board members come prepared. Facilitate a workshop designed to get them to share. The presenters should be the clients, not you. You are asking them to tell you their problems. You are hunting for obstacles standing in the way of their success. Be sure to create an opportunity for the clients to talk to one another. Make it worthwhile for them to participate. And wrap some client entertainment around it to make it fun.

Next, it is wise to implement postproject reviews. This is an assessment of project results, activities, and processes. It is conducted by an employee who was not on the project team. This person interviews each project team member. They review project objectives, profitability, timelines, budgets, deliverables, and adherence to standard operating procedures. A report is produced. As this is done for every project, a valuable archive is built up. This often highlights new offerings worth considering.

Next, a formal client satisfaction program is implemented. Boutiques that successfully scale make this mandatory. Upon completion of a project, the client personnel receive a questionnaire. The tool invites the client to evaluate the firm on a set of dimensions. The results often reveal ideas for new services. This is frequently outsourced to a third party that specializes in the professional services industry. Be careful. Popular tools, such as Net Promoter Score, are not particularly useful for boutiques. They tend to be too generic and easily manipulated.

Next, focus on new clients. Implement a win-loss program. This program will deconstruct why you win, and lose, new clients. It is from the perspective of the prospect. It typically takes place once per quarter and is often outsourced. A group of recent campaigns are batched up. An objective third party calls the prospects and asks probing questions. The results are aggregated and then tabulated. Over time, boutiques can benchmark themselves and spot trends. Very often the losses reveal holes in the service offering.

Lastly, I recommend attending conferences. Not conferences for your industry but the conferences that your clients attend. Most industries have a few must-see conferences. Clients go to these conferences looking for answers to their problems. Much can be learned from reading the agenda. The conference coordinators put these agendas together for maximum relevance. The talks are often given by your clients or their competitors. This is an opportunity to get insight directly from the horse's mouth. I used to spend considerable time walking the trade show floor. These vendors paid good money to pitch their wares. I used to approach them and ask, "What problem do you solve?" By the end of a couple of days, I would leave with pages of ideas for new offerings.

Should you invest in expanding your offerings?

Answer these questions to find out:

1. Is your growth dependent on increasing revenue from existing clients?

   ☐ yes ☐ no

2. Do you need new reasons to remain relevant to your clients?

   ☐ yes ☐ no

3. Do your clients eventually get fatigued?

   ☐ yes ☐ no

4. Do you know what your clients need?

   ☐ yes ☐ no

5. Can you continuously learn what your clients need?

   ☐ yes ☐ no

6. Would your clients participate on a client advisory board?

   ☐ yes ☐ no

7. Can you implement postproject reviews?

   ☐ yes ☐ no

8. Can you perform client satisfaction reviews after every project?

   ☐ yes ☐ no

9. Can you perform win-loss reviews after every sales campaign?

   ☐ yes ☐ no

10. Are there relevant industry conferences that you can attend?

    ☐ yes ☐ no

If you answered yes to eight or more of these questions, you have an opportunity. You can scale by bringing new service offerings to market.

If you answered no to eight or more of these questions, you do not have an opportunity. You are unlikely to scale from new service offerings.

## SUMMARY

If you have one thing to sell and deliver, scale will be hard. Expand your offerings. Increase your addressable market. Be more valuable to your clients. Accelerate scale through service offering expansion.

## CHAPTER 20

# THE CLIENT EXPERIENCE

As start-ups evolve into boutiques, they begin to serve different clients. These clients tend to be more sophisticated and have higher expectations. Boutiques that do not recognize this, and adjust, fail to scale. The client experience becomes mission critical.

What do I mean when I say *client experience*?

Allow me to share a story to illustrate.

A website design firm has been in business for a few years. Their clients are midsize companies looking to redesign aging websites. This boutique's differentiation is its unique combination of creative and technical talent. They have been stuck at about thirty people for a couple of years. Growth has flatlined. Scale is illusive. Owners are frustrated.

Seeking to learn why, they launch a client satisfaction program. The results reveal the issue. The clients' expectations have changed, and the boutique has not changed with them. Delivering quality work is no longer enough. The clients want great service as well.

They ask me, "What is the difference between quality and service?"

The difference is subtle but impactful. In this case, many boutiques can build quality websites. Quality is measured by the finished product. For instance, does the site function well and is it easy to navigate?

**Service is measured by how the client feels while working with you.**

However, few website design firms service clients well. Service is measured by how the client feels while working with you. For instance, does your boutique take the time to explain things? Does the client understand what you are doing and why you are doing it? In other words, do your clients feel like just another client? Or do they feel special?

Clients are people, and people are emotional creatures. Hiring and working with a boutique is an emotional roller-coaster ride. Boutiques that scale recognize this and design the client experience around it. For instance, here is a subset of the client's emotions when working with you:

- Threatened: This firm is encroaching on my space.
- Worried: Will this firm make me look bad?
- Ignorant: I am supposed to know this stuff. These guys make me feel stupid.
- Concerned: These guys don't know my company or industry.
- Suspicious: Can these guys be trusted?
- Skeptical: Is this going to work?
- Exposed: These guys have access to my boss? Uh-oh.
- Insecure: I have never hired a firm like this. Am I making a

good decision?

The boutique trying to scale must manage the client in this context. It is not enough to deliver quality work. Client service must be exceptional when dealing with more sophisticated clients.

Professional services are consumed over time. The signing of a contract is the beginning, not the end. Can you sustain an exceptional client experience throughout the duration of the project? Will the client feel special at week twenty-three? The client will really get to know you. Boutiques struggling to scale make a great first impression and then fade. This results in low share of wallet and insufficient referral generation.

The solution to this problem is to implement a client experience program. The literature on client experience design can be overwhelming. I will do my best to provide you with the basics here. The following elements are appropriate for a boutique trying to scale:

1. Modify client satisfaction programs to include service in addition to quality.
2. Add client experience feedback to every postproject review. Engage team members. Behavior will change only if they are aware of the issue.
3. Add the client experience journey to the methodologies used to deliver work. Lay the emotional roller coaster on top of the standard operating procedures and the operating manuals.
4. Train the team on the client experience. Teach them how to deliver outstanding service.
5. Include client experience feedback in employee performance reviews. Bonuses and promotions go to those who excel at

this critical scale initiative.

Here are some questions to consider. They will help diagnose whether client experience is an issue.

1. Have you documented the client experience journey?

   ☐ yes ☐ no

2. Do each of your clients feel that they are important to you?

   ☐ yes ☐ no

3. Do you understand the emotional context of the client during an engagement?

   ☐ yes ☐ no

4. Do clients know why you are doing what you are doing?

   ☐ yes ☐ no

5. Do clients feel that they are part of the engagement team?

   ☐ yes ☐ no

6. Do clients know what is going to happen next before it happens?

   ☐ yes ☐ no

7. Do you research meeting attendees prior to each meeting?

   ☐ yes ☐ no

8. Do you send prereading material to clients in enough time?

   ☐ yes ☐ no

9. Do you make it easy for clients to use your materials internally?

   ☐ yes ☐ no

10. Do you call the client after every meeting to confirm that goals were met?

    ☐ yes ☐ no

If you answered yes to eight or more of these questions, you likely provide good service. Congratulations.

If you answered no to eight or more of these questions, consider a client experience program. It may be preventing you from scaling.

## SUMMARY

Quality work is a commodity. This is tough to hear. You are proud of what you produce. And you should be. It took you years to develop your expertise. However, some clients are not capable of recognizing your brilliance. And you are not the only firm providing quality work. Boutiques that break out and scale understand that the client experience is more important. Far fewer firms can deliver outstanding service in addition to quality work. This is the unique differentiator to develop.

## CHAPTER 21

# ORGANIZATIONAL STRUCTURE

Organizational design is easy as a start-up. There are three boxes: marketing/sales, service delivery, and service development. However, a one-hundred-person boutique needs to think about organizational structure. Key questions must be answered:

- How many people do I need?
- What type of people do I need?
- Which organizational structure is best for me?

Labor is the biggest expense for a boutique. Therefore, it has the biggest impact on profitability. Too much work and not enough people results in burnout and turnover. Too little work and too many people results in employees on the bench and poor profits. The ability to match supply and demand is key to scaling a

**The ability to match supply and demand is key to scaling a boutique.**

boutique.

The up-or-out pyramid model is the most deployed. This was popularized by David Maister twenty-seven years ago. The market leaders—that is, the 4,100—use a version of it. Here is a simplified explanation.

At the top of the pyramid are the finders. These are the partners mainly responsible for finding clients. In the middle of the pyramid are the minders. These are the managers primarily responsible for managing engagements. At the bottom of the pyramid are the grinders. These are junior employees who complete task-level work.

New employees are recruited into the bottom of the pyramid. They become grinders for a specified period. This can range from one to five years depending on firm policy. The capable move up to the middle of the pyramid and become minders. The underperformers are managed out. This is where the term *up or out* originated.

Minders spend a period in the middle, which is also typically one to five years depending on firm policy. The capable move up to the top of the pyramid. They become finders. The underperformers are managed out. Reaching the top of the pyramid usually comes with the title of partner. Partners stay at firms for entire careers. They get managed out of the pyramid upon retirement or when they leave voluntarily.

This model has several advantages. For instance, it provides a pipeline of talent to meet future demand. Employee productivity is very high as job standards are established. Underperformers are pushed out to make way for new blood. Employees have a clear career path. It is easy for owners to manage. For instance, a firm growing at 30 percent needs 30 percent more employees. And the leverage ratios dictate the number needed for each role. Tenure bands fit nicely in spreadsheet models. The implementation of this model has resulted in many firms scaling.

However, this model has several disadvantages. For instance, it leads to a firm with a lot of employees. Revenue growth and people growth are linear. And, as you well know, more people equals more problems. It also assumes that impatient young employees will stay in a role for years. Many will not and quit, which spikes turnover. In addition, it requires that most, if not all, new employees are recent graduates. New employees enter at the bottom of the pyramid. This prevents, or limits, a firm's ability to bring in senior talent. And this model makes it very difficult to push equity ownership into the ranks.

These are but just a few of the pros and cons of this approach. However, I suggest that this model is outdated. Boutiques that are looking to scale are best served to think differently.

How?

Decouple the rate of revenue growth with the rate of employee growth. This is done by reengineering the way a service is delivered. As of this writing, this is happening primarily in three ways.

First, services are becoming tech enabled. For example, many wealth management firms rely on robo advisers. These machines perform services that humans previously did. Most financial plans and asset allocation decisions are now down by algorithms. This allows wealth management firms to acquire clients without having to add employees.

Second, offshoring labor. For example, many IT service providers offshore work to India. These emerging countries often produce better work for a fraction of the cost. This trend started in IT but is accelerating in every function. Market leaders, the 4,100, offshore about 40 percent of their work. Boutiques offshore less than 5 percent. Owners of boutiques who get good at labor arbitrage will scale nicely. And profit handsomely.

Third, leveraging gig networks. For example, management consulting firms leverage labor marketplaces. The most popular is Catalant. Its marketplace is comprised of thousands of freelancers, many formerly employed by brand-name firms. Boutiques can use these marketplaces to flex up and flex down when needed. This allows a boutique to be much more flexible when trying to match revenue and expenses.

The up-or-out pyramid still has value. And it may make sense for you to adopt your version of it. But do so after you have engineered your services. Many boutiques have too many people. Many of them are employees with outdated skills. The amount of time it takes to manage a large employee base is not insignificant. This model is slow. And the world is moving fast. It used to be that the best boutiques were those with a lot of employees. That is no longer true. The best boutiques are those with a lot of free cash flow. The fewer the employees, the better.

Here are some questions to help you think through organizational design:

1. Can you decouple the rate of revenue growth from the rate of employee growth?

   ☐ yes ☐ no

2. Are most of your problems people related?

   ☐ yes ☐ no

3. Is payroll your biggest expense?

   ☐ yes ☐ no

4. Can technology perform work that humans are doing today?

   ☐ yes ☐ no

5. Are you offshoring less than 40 percent of your work?

   ☐ yes ☐ no

6. Can you flex up/flex down head count to match demand close to real time?

   ☐ yes ☐ no

7. Are you skilled at labor arbitrage?

   ☐ yes ☐ no

8. Is it clear that scale does not refer to the number of employees but to the amount of cash flow?

   ☐ yes ☐ no

9. Is it hard to match revenue and expenses?

   ☐ yes ☐ no

10. Do you have limited forward visibility in your business?

   ☐ yes ☐ no

If you answered yes to eight or more of these questions, it is time for you to reorganize. It may unlock trapped scale inside your firm.

If you answered no to eight or more of these questions, stick with your current organizational structure.

## SUMMARY

The best boutique would have no employees and many clients. Labor is your biggest cost. Organize to reduce employee-related expenses. This will drive profits up. The rigid up-or-out pyramid must be modernized. The next generation of market leaders will be those who organize creatively.

CHAPTER 22

# RECRUITING

Marshall Goldsmith once wrote, "What got you here won't get you there." In my experience, he is correct. The fact is that the people on your organizational chart need to change over time. Recruiting shows up on the list of things to excel at during this phase. The days of recruiting from your personal network are over. The ability to recruit at scale separates market leaders from boutiques.

**The ability to recruit at scale separates market leaders from boutiques.**

There are four different recruiting needs when scaling:

1. *Replace generalists with specialists.* As you scale, you will attract sophisticated clients. These clients will pay more and will therefore expect more. They are experienced purchasers of professional services. Your proposals will need to specify the experience levels and work histories of your team. You will not get away with "engagement with manager with five years of experience." You will need to state, "EM, 10 years' experience in x industry, y segment, z project type." The need to recruit specialists spikes when scaling.

2. *Manager of managers*. Start-ups are filled with small teams. Boutiques are filled with medium-size teams. Market leaders are filled with large teams. Start-ups hire managers who manage individuals. Boutiques hire managers who manage managers. Market leaders hire managers who manage departments. You will need to recruit, or develop, managers of managers during scale. At about midsize, the need for a manager of managers shows up.

3. *Executives*. Boutiques at scale require executive leadership teams. These executives have autonomy to make decisions. They are not simply implementing the plans made by the founder. They are drafting their own plans. Often they run their own P&L, giving them spending authority. Start-ups, in contrast, have managers. When transitioning from start-up to boutique, augment managers with executives. The need to recruit an executive leadership team arrives when scaling.

4. *Reassign the founder*. Founders are bold risk-takers with visions of the future that others cannot see. These pioneers are the job creators and the wealth creators. They have a remarkable ability to learn. And they understand that just because things are uncertain, they are not risky. Founders do not become paralyzed by what they do not know. There is a reason why we celebrate the Jeff Bezoses of the world. They are our heroes. However, at a certain point, founders become a bottleneck. Founders want to launch new services, enter new markets, and innovate. They do not want to install process, systems, and scale. Yet that is what is needed during the scale stage. Therefore, founders must hire or promote a new CEO. By doing so, they can amplify their impact. The objective is not for the founder to stop working or

> to work less. Rather, it is to make the founder's contributions much more impactful. The CEO runs today's business while the founder is developing tomorrow's business. The one-two punch accelerates the pace of scaling.

I was a founder, and here is what happened to me. I sold my boutique, SBI, in 2017. An exceptional executive, Matt Sharrers, became CEO upon my departure. Matt replaced leading by intuition with leading by data. He recruited specialists, managers of managers, and an executive leadership team. SBI no longer needed an inspirational vision or a big dream to chase. It needed flawless execution of the existing business model. SBI needed to scale. This required replacing me the founder with Matt the CEO.

The results were remarkable. Matt increased the enterprise value of the firm. And sold it again at the end of 2019, creating wealth for all stakeholders.

This accomplishment is very rare. It is more common that a boutique shrinks when the founder leaves. And almost never are there two successful exits in three years. It is very hard to exit once. To do it twice is remarkable. And do it twice in three years is unheard of.

This is what can happen when the founder is replaced at the right time.

Do you need a new recruiting strategy?

1. Do individual contributors need to evolve into managers?

   ☐ yes ☐ no

2. Do managers need to evolve into managers of managers?

   ☐ yes ☐ no

3. Do managers of managers need to evolve into executives?

   ☐ yes ☐ no

4. Do you need to shift from generalists to specialists?

   ☐ yes ☐ no

5. Are you attracting sophisticated clients with higher expectations?

   ☐ yes ☐ no

6. Has the founder become a bottleneck?

   ☐ yes ☐ no

7. Can the impact of the founder be amplified if partnered with a CEO?

   ☐ yes ☐ no

8. Does decision-making need to get pushed to those closest to the clients?

   ☐ yes ☐ no

9. Is it time to shift from experimenting with the model to scaling the model?

   ☐ yes ☐ no

10. Is it true that "what got you here won't get you there"?

   ☐ yes ☐ no

## SUMMARY

Recruiting as a start-up is not a mission-critical task. The needs are basic, and most jobs can be filled from personal networks. In contrast, recruiting at scaling is a mission-critical task. The job requirements are much more demanding. The jobs often cannot be filled from personal networks. Specialists, managers, and executives need to be formally recruited. And this can include the recruiting of a CEO to replace/complement the founder.

CHAPTER 23

# PARTNER PAY

Boutiques grow. This means that they are implementing a new organizational model. At the top of the chart, there is this role called partner. There are more and more of them over time. A new role, growing in count, requires special attention. CEOs need a system for partner pay.

Why?

A boutique requires different things from its partners as it scales. For example, partners might need to recruit employees. Or they may need to develop junior staff. Maybe they are placed in charge of a new specialty industry practice. In some cases, a partner is sent overseas to open the international operation. The days of just selling and delivering work are over. Firm-building activities become part of a partner's job description. It is no longer just about personal billings. How should partners be compensated for these activities?

**A boutique requires different things from its partners as it scales.**

There are two components to these systems:

1. Salaries
2. Bonuses

Salaries are easy. Simply determine the role. Calculate the going rate in the market for the role. Pay at the midpoint. For instance, a business development partner earns a $126,000 salary, according to salary.com. Benchmark salary data is widely available. Pick your source. The reason to pay at the midpoint is simple. A boutique is not a start-up, nor is it a large market leader. It is at the midpoint. You can tweak this up or down as you see fit. However, the main point is to pay according to the market rate. Partners are labor. Labor is a commodity priced in the open market. There are buyers and sellers for this labor. The equilibrium point between a buyer and a seller is the price of the commodity. If the partner quit your boutique, this is what they would fetch. If you recruited a new partner, this is what you would pay. Eliminate the subjectivity from salary discussions. Relay on market-based salary figures.

Let's now turn to bonuses. Determining the bonus payouts for partners is more difficult.

Paying bonuses at boutiques is very different from paying bonuses at large firms. The reason is because of the number of partners at big firms. It is not uncommon for market leaders to have hundreds of partners. Some firms have different levels of partners (junior partner, senior partner, etc.). Therefore, each partner's piece of the profit pie is small.

Boutiques have far fewer partners than big firms. The share of the profit pool is larger for each partner. And it is more important to pay bonuses correctly at boutiques. It has a disproportionally bigger impact on the firm and on the partner.

The key issue in bonus calculation is balance. It is important to reward current contributions. And it is important to recognize long-term contributions. Which gets weighted more?

The cleanest way to calculate bonuses is the impact on wealth creation. Partners are owners. An owner's job is to create wealth for themselves and for the other owners. Wealth is created at a boutique in two ways:

1. Increasing EBITDA
2. Increasing the multiple placed on EBITDA

For example, a hypothetical firm has $5 million in EBITDA. The firm could fetch ten times EBITDA in the open market. Therefore, the firm is worth $50 million. Through the partner's efforts, they add $1 million in EBITDA. This partner created $10 million in wealth for the firm. How much of that should they get?

Or, let's say that at this same firm, a partner does something remarkable. And this remarkable accomplishment results in the multiple going from ten times to eleven times. The firm is now worth $55 million instead of $50 million. The partner created $5 million in wealth. How much of that should they get?

There are three systems that boutiques should consider when determining bonuses. Each has its pros and cons. Consider the following and decide which is best for you.

First is the seniority system. Increases in bonuses are formulaic and tied to years of service. The pros of this approach are easy to understand. The partner's past efforts are contributing to the firm's current profitability. Their years of experience help win new business. This system is focused on the long term. It avoids the problems with year-over-year performance swings. It is easy to administer and understand. And there is no time wasted bickering about who should get what.

The cons are also easy to understand. The partner's past contributions may have ceased to benefit the firm. This system may result in high turnover with young superstars. They do not want to wait around while the old guys get rich. And how do rewards get distributed among partners with the same seniority?

Next are the performance-based systems. Partnership profits are divided according to objective performance measures. Typical measures are the origination of business, yield, and project profitability. The advantage of this system is obvious. It is clear-cut. Hit the goals and get paid. Miss the goals and go without.

There are numerous problems with this approach. For example, in this system there is no incentive to build the firm. Referrals are not rewarded. Nor is developing staff. Leverage suffers, as partners want to drive up personal billability. Instead of off-loading work to juniors, they hoard the billings. Why develop a new practice if it won't pay off this year? Pay that prioritizes short-term performance can destroy a boutique's ability to scale.

Third is the reconciliation system. The partners distribute profits after reconciling how wealth was created for one another. The partners are the jury. This way the system has integrity. A methodology is developed and followed consistently. Evidence of wealth creation is collected. Bonus calculations come with detailed explanations of the logic.

The pros of this approach are many. Contribution to wealth creation is the single criterion. This balances the short term and the long term. There are few fights over partner pay, as each partner is on the jury. The legitimacy and integrity of the system is sound. There are no miscommunication problems and no politics. There is no king ruling over this critical decision. All partners have a voice, and there are checks and balances. Difficult trade-offs can be made through compromise. It sends a clear signal as to what is valued in the firm. The bonus formula is not set in stone. It can change with time and keep pace with the evolution of the boutique. It forces each partner to critically assess how they are spending their time. If an activity is not linked to wealth creation, why do it? This approach prevents boutiques from chasing the new shiny object. Careful planning happens before any new initiative is launched. It eliminates paying the title and requires paying the contribution. Bonuses are not automatic. They must be earned. This system prevents coasting, as bonuses are recalculated every year.

There are some cons to this system. Attributing a partner's activities to wealth creation can, at times, be difficult. Partners at boutiques are inexperienced and may make mistakes. Sometimes they do not have all the facts and confuse correlation with causation. It can be time consuming, as it requires strategic thought. As boutiques scale and add more partners, there could be too many chefs in the kitchen. Not all partners are comfortable sharing opinions in an open forum. Reconciling quantitative and qualitative data in a consistent way is challenging. It is not foolproof, nor is it 100 percent precise. Rather, it is the collective judgment of the entire partnership. This system requires full disclosure. Every partner knows how much the other got.

I would like to share some personal experiences with you that should help. As I transitioned from start-up to boutique, I did not change the partner compensation system. This cost me millions of dollars over time, and it created tension among the partners.

Our system was unsophisticated. We paid partners a very generous salary that was not market based. The first group of partners was earning two times what they could fetch in the open market. Bonuses were paid as distributions. The distributions were paid based on the partners' equity stake. For example, if a partner owned 25 percent of the firm, they got 25 percent of the distributions. This was a mistake. Changing equity stakes is much harder than changing bonus payouts. The rigidity of this system was very limiting.

The root cause of these mistakes is easy to identify. I felt a loyalty to the early partners. They took a big risk to join me. They took equity in the firm instead of cash in the early days. As we became successful, I wanted to reward them for the early sacrifices. However, I did not consider when this "debt" was paid. I just kept paying the debt in perpetuity. They took advantage of me. The right thing to do would have been to refuse the excessive compensation. But greed and envy are powerful forces for humans to resist. And I am sure that they felt they deserved what they were getting. All of us, including me, tend to overstate our true worth.

The result was that the new group of partners was undercompensated. The effect they were having on the business was large and growing. Eventually it eclipsed the contribution from the legacy partners. And as time went on, this compounded. The contribution gap between the legacy and the new partners became extreme. The dollars should have shifted to the new partners. Yet they did not. This was a failure of leadership by me. This poor leadership fractured relationships. And it created some bad blood. I regret this. Friends became enemies, sadly. The shame of it all is that this is avoidable. I just did not know any better. I wish this book had been available then. This all could have been prevented. Please learn from my mistakes. Maybe my salvation can be realized in helping you steer clear of this grief.

Are you adding partners and need a new way to pay them?

Here are a few questions to think through:

1. Are you paying salaries based on external benchmarks?

   ☐ yes ☐ no

2. Are you paying salaries at the midpoint of the benchmarks?

   ☐ yes ☐ no

If you answered yes to questions 1 and 2, you do not need a new partner pay system.

If you answered no to questions 1 and 2, you should consider a new partner pay system.

3. Are years of service a fair way to pay partners?

   ☐ yes ☐ no

4. Are senior partners' past contributions contributing to today's wealth creation?

   ☐ yes ☐ no

5. Will the younger partners stick around to wait for the senior partners to retire?

   ☐ yes ☐ no

If you answered yes to questions 3, 4, and 5, a seniority-based system might work.

If you answered no to questions 3, 4, and 5, a seniority-based system is not for you.

6. Do you have clear objectives for each partner?

   ☐ yes ☐ no

7. Is it clear when the objectives are met?

   ☐ yes ☐ no

8. Is it possible to balance short-term and long-term wealth

creation with these objectives?

☐ yes ☐ no

If you answered yes to questions 6, 7, and 8, consider a performance-based system.

If you answered no to questions 6, 7, and 8, a performance-based system is not right for you.

9. Will partners perform with integrity if placed on the bonus jury?

   ☐ yes ☐ no

10. Can you develop a methodology that fairly attributes wealth creation to partner activities?

    ☐ yes ☐ no

If you answered yes to questions 9 and 10, a reconciliation system might work.

If you answered no to questions 9 and 10, a reconciliation system will not work.

## SUMMARY

Boutiques add more partners over time. Paying partners correctly impacts the scalability of the boutique. It requires strategic thinking. Getting it wrong results in a destruction of wealth. Getting it right results in the creation of wealth.

## CHAPTER 24

# EQUITY

There are many ways to split up a partnership. And the equity split among partners needs to evolve over time. Allow me to share a story to illustrate.

Three friends founded a real estate appraisal firm. They specialized in appraising land and commercial buildings. They were hired by the banks that were providing the mortgages. They were hired by insurance companies when insuring the properties. And they were hired by divorce attorneys to assess the value of an estate to be divided up.

When they founded the firm, they split the equity equally. Each partner received one-third of the shares. The business started slow but grew nicely. The first few years were filled with fun, and everyone got along. However, as the years passed, some resentment crept in. In particular, the success of one partner was far greater than the success of other two. This partner began to feel that he was not being treated fairly. He wanted to be rewarded for his outsize contributions to the partnership. The partners were taking quarterly distributions. It bothered him when the excess profits went to the other two partners. He felt that they did not deserve them. In addition, this partner wanted to scale the firm. He proposed to redirect profit distributions back into the business. This was to be used to hire additional staff and invest in marketing. This was met with resistance. The other two partners were happy with a lifestyle business. They did not see the benefit of scaling and did not want the headache. Adding to the problem was the age discrepancy. The aggressive partner was in his early forties. The passive partners were in their early sixties. The aggressive partner had his children's college bills to pay for. The passive partners wanted to ease into retirement. Different life stages drove different motivations and financial needs.

The situation deteriorated and became hostile. The aggressive partner threatened to quit and take the clients and the key staff. The passive partners threatened to sue. Their accountant suggested a buyout, whereby the aggressive partner would buy out the passive partners. A valuation firm was hired. A value was placed on the shares. The partners disagreed with how the valuation was determined. They could not agree on a price. And they could not agree on the terms of a deal. The oldest partner was having some health issues. He wanted to be paid in full at closing. The youngest partner offered no up-front cash and a five-year earn-out. On and on the negotiations went.

In the end, a private lender sponsored a management buyout. The young partner borrowed the money to buy out the older partners. The financing terms were favorable, and the lender agreed to waive a personal guarantee. The debt service was manageable, so the young partner, now CEO, agreed. He felt that he could grow the business, pay off the loan, and emerge with 100 percent of a great firm. The older partners got a nice payout and a fully funded retirement. After a lot of hard feelings, in the end, everyone got what they wanted. It took a few years, but I am happy to report that the fences have been mended. These once great friends are friends once again.

What is the moral of this story?

Equity arrangements must be flexible. What worked as a start-up does not work as a boutique. And as a boutique scales, equity splits must be modified.

This story had a happy ending, but many do not. Many boutiques have been ruined because of disagreements over equity. When a firm starts, it is almost impossible to value it correctly. There are no clients, revenue, intellectual property, or profit. One hundred percent of zero is equal to $0. And partner contributions to wealth creation change over time. Therefore, fixed equity arrangements are discouraged.

**Many boutiques have been ruined because of disagreements over equity.**

The best solution to this problem is to prevent it from happening in the first place. When you start the firm, value it solely on contributed capital. For instance, let's say a boutique requires $1 million to get started. There are three partners. One partner contributes $500,000 and owns 50 percent of the firm. The second partner contributes $300,000 and owns 30 percent of the firm. The third partner contributes $200,000 and owns 20 percent of the firm. This is clean and clear-cut. Do not award ownership based on sweat equity. Sweat equity is impossible to value when calculating ownership percentages. For instance, what percentage of ownership should be given to a great rainmaker versus a good rainmaker? The question is too difficult to try to answer. Instead, sweat equity is accounted for in salaries. For instance, if a partner is responsible for project management, they get paid as a project manager would. That is the value of the role, and it is set objectively by the open market.

If an equity split problem does emerge as you scale, there is a solution. It is called a buy-sell agreement. This is a contract that stipulates how a partner's share of a business can be bought and sold. It defines how such a process will work. It prevents expensive litigation. The agreement should include a business valuation clause. This specifies that a business valuation expert will assess the appropriate way to value the business. A common mistake made by boutiques is predetermining a valuation formula. For instance, two times trailing twelve months' revenue. This may or may not represent the true value of the firm. It is best to develop the agreement before it is needed. This reduces the emotional impact of these decisions. These agreements should include some basic ground rules. For example, it might specify how a purchase of equity can be funded. Or it might specify how a sale can be triggered. Often it makes sense to consult with a tax adviser when drafting the agreement. There are ways to structure these to limit how much goes to Uncle Sam.

Unfortunately, very few boutiques have buy-sell agreements in place. They do not think that they need them. It has been my experience that every boutique should have one. Equity splits will need to change over time. The contributions to wealth creation made by each partner will change over time. It is important that rewards are representative of contributions.

Find out if your partnership is split up correctly.

1. Is your firm owned by more than one person?

   ☐ yes ☐ no

2. Do the owners contribute to wealth creation in different proportions?

   ☐ yes ☐ no

3. Are the owners at different stages in life?

   ☐ yes ☐ no

4. Do the owners have different financial needs?

   ☐ yes ☐ no

5. Do the owners have different visions of the future?

   ☐ yes ☐ no

6. Have the partner contributions fluctuated over the years?

   ☐ yes ☐ no

7. Has resentment crept into the relationships?

   ☐ yes ☐ no

8. Are you living with a legacy ownership structure that is now outdated?

   ☐ yes ☐ no

9. Will rising stars require ownership to be retained?

   ☐ yes ☐ no

10. Has the ownership structure distorted policy making?

    ☐ yes ☐ no

If you answered yes to eight or more of these questions, it is time to rethink ownership.

If you answered no to eight or more of these questions, equity splits are not preventing scale.

## SUMMARY

Converting income into wealth is how boutique owners realize their dreams. Generating a high W2 or K1 is easy. Building a large balance sheet is hard. Net worth trumps net income. And net worth is generated from ownership. Be sure that your scaling efforts produce a lot of personal wealth. This requires the right ownership structure.

# CHAPTER 25
# POWER

As boutiques scale, the way decisions are made must change. The power shifts from the dictator to the team.

Start-up professional services firms require a dictator to be successful. The firm does not have time to build consensus. It must rapidly iterate and move quickly to be successful. The scope of the decisions that need to be made is small. The personal willpower of the dictator is a key reason for success. Strong leadership is crucial to the success of the start-up. The skills needed in the dictator are easily defined and readily available.

At some point along the way, the boutique needs to implement a democracy. The boutique is larger, and leadership must represent the team. More people need to have a say. The dictator is removed from the front lines. Their proximity to the client becomes more distant. As a result, their decision-making ability becomes diminished. This person's once prophetic instincts become dulled.

Democracies mean less centralized power and more autonomy for the team. The nature of a boutique requires this approach. Clients turn to boutiques because they want to feel important. Boutiques make clients feel special in how they interact with them. For instance, a service may be customized by a boutique for a specific client. Boutiques must be less hierarchal so that they can be responsive. This requires power to be pushed down to the front lines. To a degree, partners need to be able to practice as they see fit.

The best practice most boutiques have adopted can be described as follows. A board of partners is elected. This board meets quarterly and makes policy decisions. This board does not run the firm but instead focuses on long-term issues. A managing partner acts like a CEO would act in a public company. This managing partner is appointed by the board of partners. The managing partner has a small staff but outsources most of the overhead functions (IT, HR, legal, etc.). There is an executive leadership team that reports to the managing partner. These partners are the department heads. And the combination of the three make up the compensation committee. They decide on salaries, bonuses, and the like. Think of it like you would the system of government in the United States. The board is the legislative branch deciding on policy issues. The managing partner is the executive branch and is running things. The compensation committee is the judicial branch. They issue judgments.

The ultimate power sits with the owners. They own the firm and say what goes. It is their capital at risk. However, boutiques trying to scale separate the role of approving and the role of decision-making. The owners cannot make every decision. The firm has gotten too big. However, they can approve or reject decisions being made by others. The elected board brings items to the owners for a ruling. It is important that this board is elected, as they represent the employees to the owners. There are term limits that typically range from two to three years. The separation of the board and the managing partner is important. It prevents too much power from sitting with one person.

The managing partner is also limited in term, which is typically three years. However, it is quite common for a managing partner to serve multiple terms. Once a good one is found, the board works hard to keep them. It is not uncommon for a managing partner to serve ten or more years. The executive leadership team runs the practices day-to-day. They report to the managing partner. The department heads who make up the executive leadership team are selected by the managing partner.

Is it time for you to consider how power is held inside your firm?

1. Have you transitioned from start-up to boutique?

   ☐ yes ☐ no

2. Are you attempting to become a market leader—that is, one of the 4,100?

   ☐ yes ☐ no

3. Do you have a dictator in place?

   ☐ yes ☐ no

4. Have the dictator's once great instincts begun to deteriorate?

   ☐ yes ☐ no

5. Have the number of decisions to be made gone up considerably?

   ☐ yes ☐ no

6. Has the complexity of the decisions to be made increased substantially?

   ☐ yes ☐ no

7. Does it make sense to distribute authority close to the client?

   ☐ yes ☐ no

8. Do the employees want a greater say in policy making?

   ☐ yes ☐ no

9. Do the owners want to delegate decision-making more?

   ☐ yes ☐ no

10. Do you have a person capable of serving as a managing partner?

    ☐ yes ☐ no

If you answered yes to eight or more of these questions, it is time for you to alter your power structure.

If you answered no to eight or more of these questions, imbalances in power are not standing in your way.

## SUMMARY

We love our founders. They had the guts to start the firm and grow it. However, growing a firm and scaling a boutique are two different things. Firms led by one-person dictators eventually plateau. There comes a point when a democracy is a better governance system.

CHAPTER 26

# STRATEGY

Boutiques trying to scale need a strategy to do so. The problem is that many think they already have a strategy, but they do not. A collection of tactics is not a strategy. And a spreadsheet filled with business plan assumptions is not either.

Here is the typical approach to strategy used by most boutiques. This represents what not to do.

Build a list of attributes that make a market attractive. These are items such as organic growth, number of companies, need for services, and so on. This produces a list of vertical industries to pursue. Segment this list into a list of clients to pursue. Cut the data one more time to produce a list of names to reach out to. Figure out which services to pitch based on the segmentation analysis. The managing partner states, "Our strategy is to target this set of clients in these industries with this set of services." The practice leads to nods of agreement. The Excel formulas look right. The data is from a reliable source. Bingo, we have a strategy.

The problem is that your competitors performed the same exercise. And they have the exact same strategy.

Here is the correct way to develop a strategy.

Start by asking, "How are we going to win?"

This shifts the strategic planning process from what to how. How are you making your firm more attractive to clients? How are you going to compete? Until these how-based questions are answered, you do not have a strategy.

Ask how we can increase our value to clients by doing the following:

1. Recruiting a higher-caliber staff than our competitors
2. Training our team better than our competitors
3. Innovating how we deliver our services
4. Focusing on the client experience more than on the deliverables produced
5. Expanding our capabilities to solve more problems
6. Specializing in new ways

A start-up can grow by doing more of what it is doing. A boutique trying to scale needs a new way of doing things. This might mean ways to raise client satisfaction. It could be how to raise prices or the skill level of the team. Maybe it is a plan to improve utilization rates. Each one of these goals is accompanied with an action plan. This action plan is owned by a single person. This person is held accountable for its success. The person is supported with funding and resources to execute. This style of strategy cuts through the blah, blah, blah. It gets to the actions to be taken. And it is this kind of strategy that boutiques use when trying to scale. It is not a simple budgeting process.

**A boutique trying to scale needs a new way of doing things.**

Look at your current strategy document. Read it and ask these questions:

1. Does it outline how the firm will develop new capabilities that the competitors do not have?

   ☐ yes ☐ no

2. Does it detail why the competitors cannot match them?

   ☐ yes ☐ no

3. Does it specify how these capabilities will be pushed into the market?

   ☐ yes ☐ no

4. Does it explain how your capital is being allocated (people, money, and time)?

   ☐ yes ☐ no

5. Does it specify how this capital allocation plan is different from the competitors?

   ☐ yes ☐ no

6. Is the strategy supported by enough client-sourced evidence?

   ☐ yes ☐ no

7. Does the strategy specify who oversees each program?

   ☐ yes ☐ no

8. Has the team been properly incented to execute the plan?

   ☐ yes ☐ no

9. Does it detail how the competitors plan to beat you?

   ☐ yes ☐ no

10. Does it specify how you plan to respond to competitor attacks?

    ☐ yes ☐ no

If you answered yes to eight or more of these questions, you do not need a new strategy.

If you answered no to eight or more of these questions, you need a new strategy.

## SUMMARY

A collection of tactics is not a strategy, nor is a financial model or an annual budget. A strategy outlining the what is not as valuable as one that outlines the how. Scaling requires strategy. Unless you consistently become more valuable to your clients, you will stall out. Stay focused on how you are going to win.

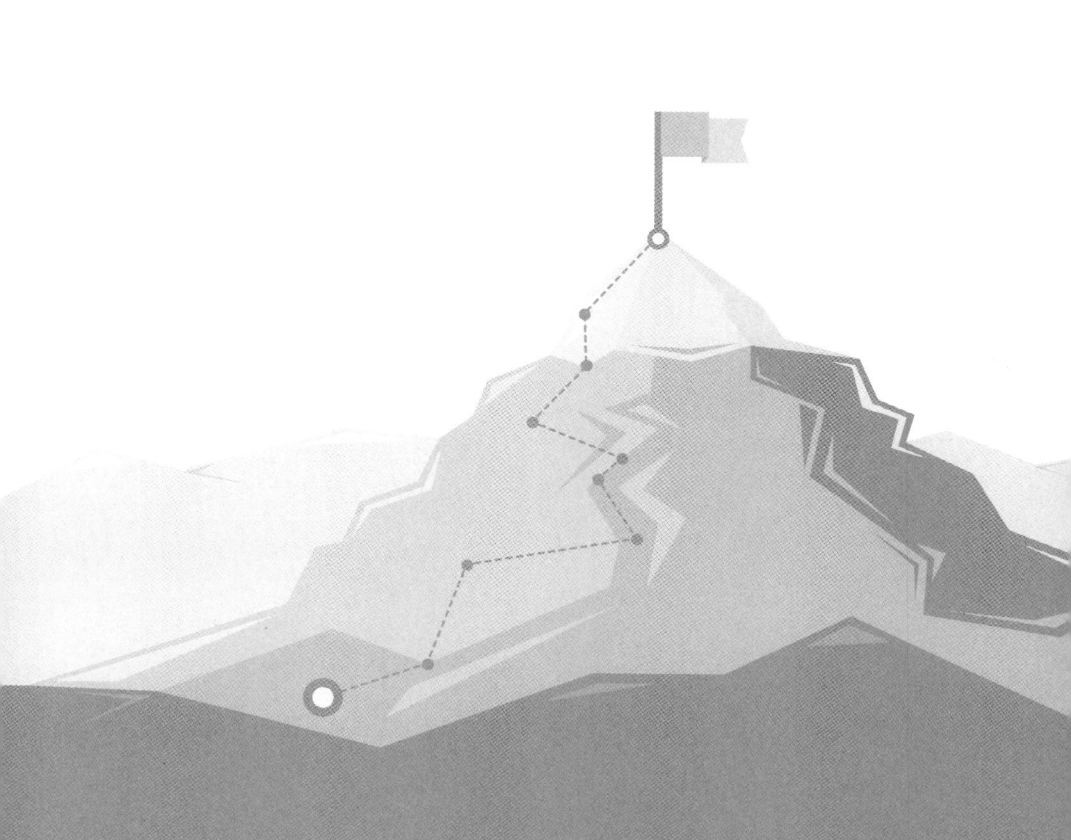

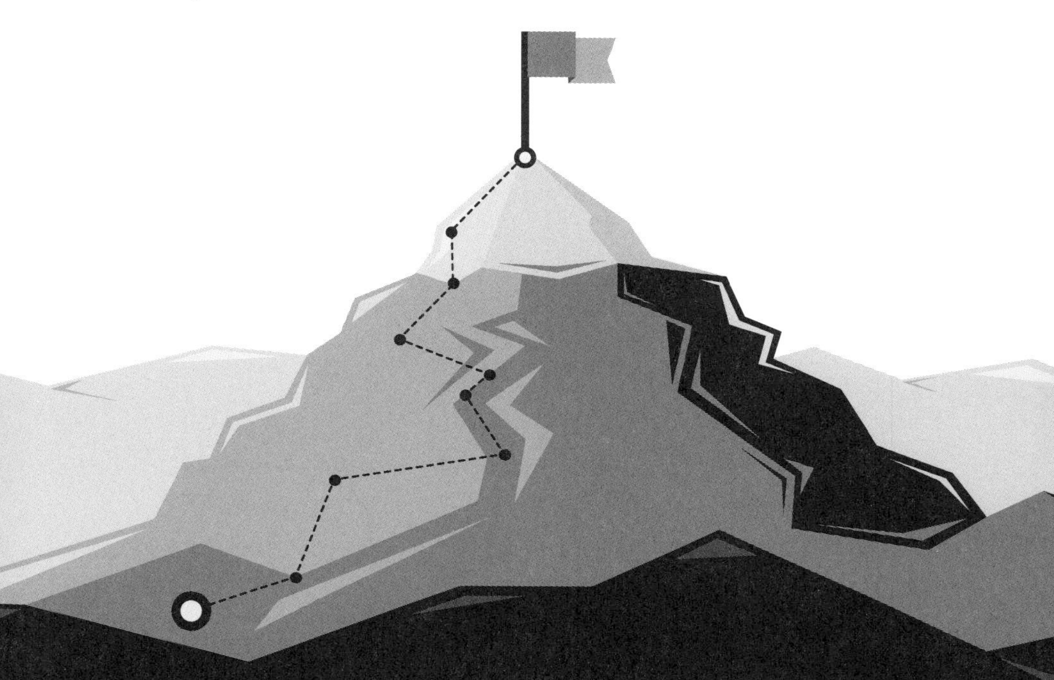

SECTION 3

# SELL

## CHAPTER 27

# WHY SELL?

The reason to sell your boutique is very personal. And it should be. You poured your life into building the firm. Leaving it—handing it to someone else—takes much thought. Some owners sell for the money. Others say they are bored; some are exhausted. And some say that the work became a job. It was not fun anymore. Some are afraid that tomorrow might not be as profitable as today. At times, partners start fighting and one needs to be bought out. Maybe it is time to retire. Or maybe you are getting divorced, and the assets are being divided. A health scare causes some to consider selling. The list is long.

I have met owners who have had happy exits. And I have met owners who have had unhappy exits.

What is the difference?

Those who had happy exits knew why they were selling. Those who had unhappy exits did not.

I am fortunate to be one of those who had a happy exit. I knew why I was selling. Allow me to share my personal journey with you. My hope is that it explains why I sold and how I came to that decision. Maybe it will help you determine whether you should sell. And if you think you want to, why you feel this way.

I first became financially independent in my twenties. I got lucky and went to work for a hot tech firm before it took off. I performed well and was rewarded with stock options. As the stock shot up, so did my personal net worth.

However, this success was not fulfilling to me. You see, I was unsure if my success was due to luck or if it was due to my ability. And I could not live with this uncertainty.

I started my firm to answer a question: "How good am I?" My thinking was that starting a firm from scratch was the purest way to find out. I started with no customers, no product, and no employees. I put all my money into the new firm and rolled the dice. If I blew it all, I was prepared to start over. If I was successful, I could look in the mirror and know what I was made of. To me, living a life without knowing what I was made of was not worth living.

Remember why you started your boutique. It helps when deciding to sell it.

As time went on, I matured. I developed a personal mission statement. I outlined a vision of my future that I wanted to pursue. I determined how I wanted to behave. I codified this into eight core values, and I lived by them. I became more spiritually aware. My political leanings and philosophical beliefs revealed themselves. And I became a skilled decision maker. I made good choices, which created new opportunities. I had met many different types of people. I learned which tribe I wanted to belong to. I discovered how best to spend my time. I knew what made me special. I knew what

**Remember why you started your boutique. It helps when deciding to sell it.**

my limitations were.

This led me to goal setting. I settled on a single goal: self-actualization. Self-actualization is part of Maslow's hierarchy of needs. It is the highest level of psychological development where the actualization of full personal potential is achieved. This occurs only after all other needs have been fulfilled. The concept of full personal potential lit a fire in my belly.

I began to evaluate my boutique against this goal. Was being the owner and CEO of this firm helping me self-actualize? The answer was no. This was hard to come to grips with. But it was true.

The firm was providing things to me that were no longer important. For example, my basic needs for food, shelter, and the like were secured for a lifetime. Safety for myself and my family was stable and certain. I had an identity outside of work. My need to belong was being fulfilled elsewhere.

And most importantly, I had answered the burning question. I had been tested. I was certain what I was made of. The firm was successful. I had become wealthy and had received plenty of recognition. I was validated internally and externally.

I had reached the point of diminishing returns. There was nothing left for me inside the boutique.

Around this time, a friend of mine gave me a book: *Halftime: Moving from Success to Significance* by Bob Buford. The big idea is how to live the second half of your life. Repeating the first half was discouraged. First-half success is no longer enough. Homes, cars, vacations, schools, and so on eventually lose their appeal. The second half is about significance. Making an impact on others, mentoring the next generation, and contributing to society becomes the second-half scorecard. This intrigued me, as I had just turned forty-seven years old. My own mortality came into my purview. The appendix of

*Halftime* is filled with extensive exercises. I put myself through them. They were designed to surface a personal definition of significance. This revealed a new plan. It was clear to me how I wanted to live my fifties, sixties, seventies, and beyond.

The plan did not include owning my boutique. In fact, it required that I sell my boutique.

My second-half plan was bold, and it needed to be funded. I now had a reason to sell.

So I sold my boutique.

I challenge you to have a happy exit. This requires you to know why you are selling.

Here are some questions to help surface your why:

1. Do you have a clear vision of your future?

   ☐ yes ☐ no

2. Does selling your boutique help you get there?

   ☐ yes ☐ no

3. Do you know why you do what you do?

   ☐ yes ☐ no

4. Would selling the firm bring you closer to your purpose?

   ☐ yes ☐ no

5. Do you have a set of values that define how you want to behave?

   ☐ yes ☐ no

6. Would the sale of your boutique allow you to behave the way you want?

   ☐ yes ☐ no

7. Do you know the type of community you want to be a part of?

   ☐ yes ☐ no

8. Would selling your firm allow you to spend time with these people?

   ☐ yes ☐ no

9. Will the proceeds of the sale fund something more than material possessions?

   ☐ yes ☐ no

10. Are you personally prepared for the next chapter of your life?

    ☐ yes ☐ no

If you answered yes to eight or more of these questions, you have a reason to sell. You should consider selling your boutique.

If you answered no to eight or more of these questions, you do not have a reason to sell. You should hold off on selling your boutique.

## SUMMARY

Every entrepreneur exits. We all die. You cannot run your boutique from the grave. Most of us sell our firms before we die. There are good exits. Some owners are happy after they sell. There are bad exits. Some owners are unhappy after they sell. Good exits start with a heartfelt, well-thought-out reason to sell.

## CHAPTER 28

# MISTAKES

Selling your boutique is a high-risk, high-reward initiative. I would like to spend some time on the common mistakes made when selling. My hope is that by reading this, you can avoid these land mines. Every situation is different; however, these are the most commonly made mistakes.

First, boutique owners are unclear as to what they want from the sale. The last chapter went into detail on how to understand why you are selling. If you are unsure of who you are, you will be unhappy with the sale. If you do not know where you are headed, you will be unhappy with the sale. There is no amount of money that will change this. After the sale is complete, there is no going back. Be sure that you know what you are doing before you start down this path.

Second, sometimes boutique owners try to sell an unsellable business. Most boutiques are unsellable. It is not enough to have a successful boutique. Your boutique needs to be attractive to a buyer. This requires you to look at your business as an investor would. An investor starts by listing all the reasons not to do a deal. The boutique owner starts with a list of all the reasons to do a deal. This gap often cannot be closed. Prior to trying to sell, be sure that you have something worth buying. A lot more on this is coming in subsequent chapters.

**Prior to trying to sell, be sure that you have something worth buying.**

Third, it takes years to sell a boutique. Yet some owners try to sell a boutique in a matter of months. This results in many failed attempts, or worse, a lot of forced sales. The process of selling takes about nine months. However, the process of preparing to sell takes two to three years. A good exit is an exit on your terms. It takes time to stack the deck in your favor. And, as they say, you have only one chance to make a first impression. It's best to be ready.

Fourth, boutique owners underinvest in succession planning. This results in seller's regret. After you sell, you will want to see your boutique do well without you. You will have many employees you care about who are still employed by the boutique. If you hand over your baby to a stranger, they may destroy it. A big bank balance does not compensate you enough for this tragedy. Spend years grooming your successor. Make sure that they build on what you have created.

Fifth, entrepreneurs think that they can sell their business on their own. This results in tactical execution errors that can cost the owner millions. Boutique owners are usually entrepreneur founders. They are very different from hired-gun CEOs. Founders have a high risk-tolerance level and supreme confidence in their abilities. They approach the selling of their business as just another problem to solve. They assume that they can figure it out. This is a mistake. And this is not an area to go cheap. Hire the best advisers that money can buy. Let these advisers guide you through the process.

Sixth, boutique owners get attacked after the sale, and they take it personally. Those who you are leaving behind will be jealous. They will feel cheated and underappreciated. They begin to tell a story that is not based in fact. Rather, it is a story they need to tell to make themselves look and feel good. Do not take it personally. This is just business. You created the wealth, and you are the one to realize it. Those who helped you along the way have benefited, and they will continue to benefit. Rest your head peacefully on the pillow at night. All that matters is what you see in the mirror.

Seventh, be sure to understand who the business is being sold to. And what their motives are. This is particularly important if you are on an earn-out or are rolling some equity. This prevents unwanted surprises from cropping up. The buyers own the asset once you sell it. They are entitled to do whatever they want with it. If you do not agree with their plans, do not sell it to them.

There are other mistakes to avoid. Every situation is different. However, these are the most common mistakes that boutique owners make.

Are you wondering if you are about to make these mistakes?

Run through these questions to find out:

1. Do you know what you want from the sale?

   ☐ yes ☐ no

2. Do you know what you are going to do after the sale?

   ☐ yes ☐ no

3. Is your business attractive to a buyer?

   ☐ yes ☐ no

4. Do you have a sellable boutique?

   ☐ yes ☐ no

5. Do you have a handpicked successor?

   ☐ yes ☐ no

6. Is the successor ready to take over?

   ☐ yes ☐ no

7. Have you lined up an all-star team of advisers to help you?

   ☐ yes ☐ no

8. Are you prepared for the postsale criticism headed your way?

   ☐ yes ☐ no

9. Do you understand who you are selling your boutique to?

   ☐ yes ☐ no

10. Do you understand their motives for buying?

   ☐ yes ☐ no

If you answered yes to eight or more of these questions, you will avoid the common mistakes made.

If you answered no to eight or more of these questions, you are likely to make some costly mistakes.

## SUMMARY

You are building a business you could run forever. You are also building a business you could sell tomorrow. If you decide to sell, you want to do so on your terms. Give yourself plenty of time to avoid these common mistakes.

# CHAPTER 29
# MARKET POSITION

An acquirer will find your boutique attractive if you are positioned well in your market. Market position is a way to determine the strength of your value proposition. A strong market position can indicate excellent competitive positioning.

There are some obvious ways to measure your market position. For instance, fee level and fee volume are two basics in any due diligence process. A fee level below $250 per hour will suggest that you are a body shop. Body shops, if they sell, typically do so for a low price. A fee level at $500 per hour will suggest that you have monetized real intellectual property. You are not selling time. Instead you are selling knowledge and skills. Boutiques such as this are capable of selling. And when they do trade, they do so at a premium price. Fee volume indicates market position by suggesting the size of the market. For instance, a fee volume of $50 million suggests a large market opportunity. It is understood that boutiques are not market leaders. Boutiques penetrate their target markets less than 10 percent. In this example, $50 million in fee volume suggests a $500+ million opportunity. Acquirers like to buy high-growth boutiques that still have a lot of runway.

In addition, there are less obvious ways to measure your market position. Savvy acquirers will consider more precise indicators of your market position. An example is client return on investment, or client ROI. Boutiques that can scale to market leaders can prove their worth to clients. Let us say that a client buys a service for $500,000 and realizes a $5 million benefit. This is a ten times return on fees charged. This is clear client ROI. In contrast, let us say that a client buys a service for $500,000 and realizes well-trained employees. This is poor client ROI. Well-trained employees are a benefit from the project. But it is not quantified, and it is not in relation to the project cost. These boutiques will not become market leaders.

**Acquirers like to buy high-growth boutiques that still have a lot of runway.**

Another way that acquirers measure a boutique's market position is call point. Call point refers to the title of the person buying the boutique's service. For instance, board members buying a boutique's service is a high call point. As is the CEO, and the CEO's direct reports. However, if the call point title is director or manager, this is a low call point. Boutiques with low call points have a hard time scaling. This is because they are selling a service not worthy of an executive's time. They are solving a problem that an executive has delegated to junior staff. This indicates that the boutique's service is not important to the clients. This will make it very hard for a boutique to scale.

Cycle resiliency is often considered by acquirers as an indicator of market position. Cycle resiliency refers to having a boutique perform in periods of recession. Recessionary periods cause clients to cut all nonessential budgets. Unfortunately, this can include discretionary budgets that many boutiques rely on. Boutiques that see steep declines in financial performance during recessions have poor market positions. Those that do well during expansions and recessions have a strong market position. It is these boutiques that have the best chance of selling their firms.

In my case, the strength of our market position was obvious. Our acquirer evaluated us through the lens of each of these attributes. And we showed well in each category. However, our cycle resiliency moved our multiple from nine times to eleven times. You see, we were founded in 2006. Many fragile young firms were wiped out during the financial crisis of 2008. Yet we pushed through this period with no problems. Looking back, this is remarkable. SBI was only three years old when the world fell apart. And we were selling a discretionary item that was easily cut by clients during tough times. But clients did not cut our services. In fact, they added to them. Our revenue and profit growth during the Great Recession was twice the rate of our peers. Our acquirer did not fear what would happen to our business during the next recession. Therefore, they paid more for it.

As you can see, market position is important to potential acquirers. It tells them whether you have compelling value propositions. It tells them how you are positioned relative to your competitors.

Do you have a strong market position?

Here some questions to help you answer this:

1. Is your average fee level about $500 per hour?

   ☐ yes ☐ no

2. If not, can you prove that you are not a body shop?

   ☐ yes ☐ no

3. Is your fee volume big enough to prove that you are in a large market?

   ☐ yes ☐ no

4. If not, can you prove that you are in a large and growing market, with a lot of runway?

   ☐ yes ☐ no

5. Do you have a clear client return on investment?

   ☐ yes ☐ no

6. If not, can you prove that your clients realize a good cost-benefit trade-off?

   ☐ yes ☐ no

7. Do you call on the board of directors of your target client?

   ☐ yes ☐ no

8. Do you call on the CEO of your target client?

   ☐ yes ☐ no

9. Did your financial performance hold up well during the last recession?

   ☐ yes ☐ no

10. Can you prove to a potential acquirer that your boutique is cycle resilient?

   ☐ yes ☐ no

If you answered yes to eight or more of these questions, you occupy a strong position in your market.

If you answered no to eight or more of these questions, you have a weak market position. It would be wise to hold off on the sales process until this is addressed.

## SUMMARY

Acquirers want to buy firms with validated market positions. This reduces their risk and increases their upside. There are many ways for a market position to be evaluated. Be sure that your case is bulletproof.

## CHAPTER 30

# GROWTH

Boutiques are attractive to potential acquirers when they are growing. And growth is determined based on growth in revenue and profits. Also, growth is relative. It is relative to the other boutiques in your space. And it is relative to the growth rates of an existing practice inside of a market leader. If your boutique is growing more and faster relative to the alternatives, you are attractive.

How do you know?

Most professional services firms are private. Therefore, data on growth rates is hard to come by. Boutiques often think that they are growing nicely, only to learn later not so much. And finding this out during due diligence is embarrassing.

I was recently involved in an auction of an IT services company. This company had a strategic relationship with the software provider Tableau. They helped clients use their data to make better decisions through data visualization. The investment bank running the auction touted the boutique as a high-growth firm. When I met with the management team, they were proud of what they had accomplished. I was presented with slide after slide of steep revenue and profit growth. And this growth was accelerating. I had looked at a few firms in this space and had an unfair information advantage. This boutique was growing revenue at 22 percent per year and had done so for about three years. The problem was that their boutique competitors were growing their top lines at twice that rate. You see, the data visualization space was hot. High water was raising all ships. When I dropped out of the bidding process, they were insulted. I explained my rationale and provided my evidence. They claimed that my comparisons were not apples to apples, that the firms I compared them to were not "pure plays." This firm was not able to find an acquirer. It appears that I was not the only one with a command of the facts. And the story gets worse. The data visualization space cooled off. Tableau, the golden goose, stopped laying eggs. As their rate of growth slowed, so did the growth rate of its service partners.

What is the moral of the story?

Know your facts. Growth is relative.

Here are a few growth benchmarks for you to consider. These are specific to NAICS 54—that is, the professional services industry. And they are specific to the segment—that is, boutiques with between 5 and 250 employees in the US. Proceed with caution. These numbers can change a lot based on the submarkets. For example, law firms are different from marketing agencies and so on.

- A five- to ten-year track record of consistent growth
- Greater than 30 percent top-line revenue growth
- More than 75 percent gross margins
- Forty percent EBITDA margins
- More than twelve months of forward visibility
- One year of payroll in cash on the balance sheet
- No debt

A boutique under five years old will have a tough time selling. One without five to ten years of solid growth in revenue and profits is unsellable. Unfortunately, many boutiques have great top-line growth but no profit growth. This is a deal killer for most. These firms have not decoupled revenue growth from head-count growth. Until they do, they should not try to sell. When they do, gross margins and EBITDA margins will jump. That is the time to sell. This is when they have a proven, scalable business model. Lastly, forward visibility must be at least a year out. Investors are not going to take your word for it. Performance relative to plan will be a much-scrutinized item.

**A boutique under five years old will have a tough time selling.**

Screen your growth against these questions:

1. Are you growing revenue faster than your boutique competitors?

   ☐ yes ☐ no

2. Have you been doing so for a few years?

   ☐ yes ☐ no

3. Are you growing your profits faster than your boutique competitors?

   ☐ yes ☐ no

4. Have you been doing so for a few years?

   ☐ yes ☐ no

5. Are you growing your revenue faster than the practice inside the large market leaders?

   ☐ yes ☐ no

6. Have you been doing so for a few years?

   ☐ yes ☐ no

7. Are you growing your profits faster than the practice inside the large market leaders?

   ☐ yes ☐ no

8. Have you been doing so for a few years?

   ☐ yes ☐ no

9. Are you growing your cash balance to cover payroll for twelve months?

   ☐ yes ☐ no

10. Do you have at least twelve months of forward visibility?

    ☐ yes ☐ no

If you answered yes to eight or more of these questions, you have an excellent growth story. You will be attractive to a buyer.

If you answered no to eight or more of these questions, your growth story needs some work. It may not be the right time to seek a sale.

## SUMMARY

Growth matters. A lot. And relative growth matters even more. A year or two of great results does not mean that you have a sellable boutique. A decade of market-beating growth will command an excellent price and excellent terms. And profit growth is as important as revenue growth. This indicates that you have cracked the code. You are one of the few who broke the link between revenue and head-count growth. Be sure to run a tight ship. Be prepared to demonstrate reliable forward visibility and plenty of working capital.

## CHAPTER 31

# CLIENT RELATIONSHIPS

A buyer is purchasing your assets. One of your assets is your client relationships. To attract the right buyer, you will need to demonstrate healthy client relationships.

How?

Acquirers will be attracted to boutiques that treat their client relationships as assets. This means that these relationships are proactively managed and scaled. Potential buyers will be turned off by boutiques that are transactional with their clients. These are firms that are reactive in their approach and neglect clients.

One area that will be placed under the microscope is revenue concentration. Many boutiques have sexy-looking financial statements. However, when you peel the cover off, you can see that they are a house of cards. They generate most of their revenue and profits from a very small number of clients. If one of these clients was to leave, the boutique's financials would fall apart. Unfortunately, this is very common, especially with project-based boutiques. These firms live and die by the big deal. Their operating model is unreliable and therefore not sellable. Be sure not to have any single client equal to more than 10 percent of billings.

Tenure of relationships is also a key item to consider. Boutiques that generate billings from clients for years are attractive. This suggests that the client relationships are strong. If the boutique did not deliver value, clients would go elsewhere. A rule of thumb is that the average client tenure should be three years or more.

An interesting personal anecdote might prove useful at this point. My firm, SBI, served sales leaders in B2B companies. The average tenure of a B2B sales leader at that time was about eighteen months. The role was a high-turnover position. I expressed to my investment banker that the tenure of our relationships was a problem. You see, when the sales leader left, our work typically stopped. And because they left every eighteen months, the tenure of our relationships was short. I was concerned that a buyer would see this and walk away from the table. The investment banker dug into the data. The data turned a negative into a positive. It revealed that the head of sales took us with them. When they took a new job, they hired our boutique at the new company. This proved that our client relationships were ironclad. It in fact, it proved that they were a real asset.

Client quality is another measure of client relationships. For instance, if your boutique generates its billings from start-ups, this will discourage buyers. Start-ups have a high failure rate. Revenue from this segment can be unreliable. In contrast, if your boutique generates its billings from the *Fortune* 500, this will encourage buyers. Large enterprises are unlikely to disappear overnight. Revenue from this segment can be reliable.

Healthy end clients are an important element to consider as well. For example, many boutiques serve the private equity community.

There are thousands of private equity firms but a smaller amount of quality firms. A boutique generates billings from private equity firms when these firms succeed. And they succeed when they can raise capital and buy companies. It is these activities that create demand for boutique services. This speaks to screening, due diligence, first hundred-day plans, and so on. Many of these activities are outsourced to boutiques. If a boutique serves low-quality private equity firms, these billings are going to dry up. These private equity firms will not be able to raise capital and will not be buying companies. As this example illustrates, healthy end clients are an important element.

Potential buyers will steer away from boutiques that do not institutionalize their relationships. Evidence of this can be found in well-documented client account plans. Buyers will want to see these account plans housed inside a customer relationship management system that is used by all. A risk that a buyer takes when buying a boutique is key employee turnover. Sometimes key client relationships sit with key employees. When the key employee leaves, they take the clients with them. Buyers will not acquire your firm if this potentiality exists. The acquirer will want to know that these relationships are with the institution and not with the employee. If the employee quits, the billings do not go away. This requires institutionalized relationship management.

How healthy are your client relationships?

1. Are your client relationships an asset on your balance sheet?

   ☐ yes ☐ no

2. Is this asset appreciating in value?

   ☐ yes ☐ no

3. Do you have a diversified client base, with no one client

worth more than 10 percent of revenue?

☐ yes ☐ no

4. Does the tenure of your client relationships exceed three years?

   ☐ yes ☐ no

5. Are your clients' businesses stable?

   ☐ yes ☐ no

6. Are your clients' end relationships stable?

   ☐ yes ☐ no

7. Do you have account plans?

   ☐ yes ☐ no

8. Have you institutionalized your client relationships into a customer relationship management system?

   ☐ yes ☐ no

9. Are the client relationships with the firm and not with the key employee?

   ☐ yes ☐ no

10. Will the billings from your client relationships stay when the key employee quits?

    ☐ yes ☐ no

If you answered yes to eight or more of these questions, you have excellent client relationships. This will make you very attractive to potential buyers.

If you answered no to eight or more of these questions, you have poor client relationships. This will make you unattractive to buyers. You are too risky for them.

## SUMMARY

Client relationships are an asset. Like other assets, some relationships appreciate in value and others depreciate. Appreciating client relationships will increase the value of your firm. Depreciating client relationships will decrease the value of your firm. When trying to exit for a great price, bulletproof your client relationships.

**When trying to exit for a great price, bulletproof your client relationships.**

# CHAPTER 32
# FEE QUALITY

In layman's terms, quality is a measure of how good, or bad, something is. The word is not often mentioned in the same sentence as fees. Yet *fee quality* is a term that boutiques looking to exit must fall in love with.

Most boutiques mistakenly think that all revenue is good revenue. This is not true. Some fee revenue is more valuable than others. For example, a boutique that generates its revenues from recurring services has high fee quality. An acquirer is willing to pay more for this type of fee than for nonrecurring revenues.

**Most boutiques mistakenly think that all revenue is good revenue. This is not true.**

What makes for high fee quality?

The first analysis of fee quality will focus on new versus existing client revenue. Boutiques that depend heavily on new-client acquisition have poor fee quality. Yes, all firms need a steady stream of new clients. However, this type of revenue is expensive to generate. And it is usually not stable. It requires heavy investment in business development. These dollars and nonbillable hours could be deployed elsewhere, generating a higher return. Also, boutiques addicted to new-client fees often are hit-and-run specialists. Some call them churn-and-burn boutiques. They perform well for a period of time. Eventually they stop growing. Word gets out that the sales pitch is better than the project delivery. This hurts new-client acquisition, the very thing they are dependent on. Boutiques that depend heavily on revenue from existing clients also have poor fee quality. It is true that firms should generate fees from existing clients. However, this type of revenue eventually disappears. The nature of boutique work is that it is temporary. Clients are renting you. At some point, they stop paying the rent. They no longer need the work to be performed, or they take it in-house. Boutiques overindexed to existing client fees forget how to hunt. They wake up one day needing new clients and cannot generate them. These boutiques often devolve into lazy lifestyle business.

High fee quality comes from a proper balance of fees from new and existing clients. A rough rule of thumb is a sixty/forty split: 60 percent of fees sources from existing clients and 40 percent of fees sourced from new clients.

The next analysis of fee quality is length of contracts. Potential buyers want to see long-term contracts with clients. For instance, a management consulting firm that performs thirty-day strategy assessments has poor fee quality. However, the boutique that performs assessments, solution development, and implementation has twelve-month client contracts. These firms have high fee quality.

After analyzing new versus existing clients, as well as length of contracts, buyers will look at fee predictability. A boutique whose services build on one another is very attractive. These boutiques often produce high fee quality due to predictability. For example, estate planning attorneys have high fee predictability. Estate plans often need updating. The attorney who writes your estate plan is very likely going to update it for you. The future fee is highly predictable. An estate plan written for a fifty-year-old changes when parents pass away. Or when grandkids arrive on the scene. Therefore, estate planning attorneys have high fee quality. The fee is predictable.

Buyers often examine fee quality based on cash collections. Boutiques that have aging accounts receivables have poor fee quality. In contrast, boutiques that are paid up front have high fee quality. Investors love firms that can use free cash flow to grow. If your boutique gets paid in advance, you are unlikely to need cash infusions. This is very attractive to financial buyers. As a rule, boutiques that rely on short-term debt to run are not attractive.

Do you have high or poor fee quality?

1. Do you generate about 60 percent of your fees from existing clients?

   ☐ yes ☐ no

2. Do you generate approximately 40 percent of your fees from new clients?

   ☐ yes ☐ no

3. Is the average client contract longer than twelve months?

   ☐ yes ☐ no

4. Do your projects naturally build on one another?

   ☐ yes ☐ no

5. Is your service built to pull through upsell?

   ☐ yes ☐ no

6. Is your service designed to pull through cross sell?

   ☐ yes ☐ no

7. Are your fees predictable?

   ☐ yes ☐ no

8. Do you collect your fee in advance of performing the work?

   ☐ yes ☐ no

9. Can you fund your growth from free cash flow?

   ☐ yes ☐ no

10. Can you pay the bills without using debt?

   ☐ yes ☐ no

If you answered yes to eight or more of these questions, you have high fee quality. You will be attractive to buyers.

If you answered no to eight or more of these questions, you have poor fee quality. This will make it difficult to sell your boutique.

## SUMMARY

All revenue is not good revenue. There are good fees, and there are bad fees. Good fees attract buyers. They increase the value of your firm. And they improve the odds of exiting. Bad fees push buyers away. They decrease the value of your firm. And they will likely to prevent you from selling your boutique.

## CHAPTER 33

# INTELLECTUAL PROPERTY

Boutiques, as a group, are confused about intellectual property. Some think that they have a lot when they do not have any. Others think that they do not have any, but they have a lot. This confusion gets cleared up when you attempt to sell your boutique. If you have real intellectual property, investors will place a value on it. If you do not, investors will not consider it in their valuation.

**If you have real intellectual property, investors will place a value on it.**

This begs the following questions: What is intellectual property? And how do boutiques create it?

Intellectual property is an invention to which one owns the rights. These rights are protected by patent, copyright, or trademark.

Boutiques create intellectual property regularly. For instance, many consultants publish books. These books are protected by copyright. Consultants turned authors receive royalty payments from their publishers. Some boutiques collect benchmark data. They then license access to this benchmarking data to clients. This benchmark data asset is protected by a licensing agreement. Boutiques often create innovative methodologies to solve certain problems. They frequently enter into licensing agreements with third parties. These third-party firms pay a licensing fee to the boutique. This grants them the right to use the methodology. If these third parties violate the licensing agreement, they can be sued. It is not uncommon for boutiques to convert their knowledge into tools. These tools are turned into software applications. The clients of these boutiques pay a per seat license to use these tools. If the application licensing agreement is in breach, the boutique can seek damages. Other boutiques create certification programs that validate someone's experience. Individuals pay boutiques to become certified in a specific skill. A popular example is PMP, project manager professional. If an individual falsifies a certification, they can be taken to court. There are many more examples.

Boutiques that have real intellectual property are selling services. They are not selling bodies. This distinction is why they are considered a professional service. Acquirers are not interested in buying subcontractor body shops. They are interested in buying professional services firms. And intellectual property is the difference.

I was advising a civil engineering firm a year ago. The owner was brilliant. He had an amazing way to hire and make profitable inexperienced engineers. This was his secret sauce. This inexperienced labor was cheap, and it allowed him to charge his clients less. As a result, he won most of the bids he submitted. He wanted to sell his firm. He hired an investment banker, and a month later, the banker fired him. He told me the banker said that his firm was not sellable. No one was going to buy it. The reason no one was going to buy it is that he had no intellectual property. He was a body shop filled with kids working for cheap. He disagreed with the banker. This brilliant entrepreneur began to explain to me his proprietary methods. They were impressive, and he was very proud of them. I interrupted and asked how these methods were protected. Were there any patents, copyrights, or trademarks? The answer was no. I then asked him if this secret sauce was generating any revenue. The answer was no. His clients were not paying for the right to use any of it. The clients were simply asking him to perform a job. And for the completion of the job, he was paid a fee. The banker was correct. He owned a body shop. He was earning a great living. But the boutique had no leverageable assets. There was nothing to really buy so that investors were interested.

A large percentage of boutiques are like this. They are great lifestyle businesses. They will produce an excellent living for the owners for years to come. And there is nothing wrong with this. However, they are not boutiques that an owner can sell. If your goal is to sell your firm, then it is important that you have intellectual property.

Do you?

Here are some questions to help you figure this out:

1. Do you have any patents?

   ☐ yes ☐ no

2. Do you have any copyrights?

   ☐ yes ☐ no

3. Do you have any trademarks?

   ☐ yes ☐ no

4. Are you generating revenue by granting the right to use your intellectual property to anyone?

   ☐ yes ☐ no

5. Are you collecting data that clients will pay to have access to?

   ☐ yes ☐ no

6. Are you inventing methodologies that third parties will pay to be able to use?

   ☐ yes ☐ no

7. Are you coding your knowledge into licensable application tools?

   ☐ yes ☐ no

8. Will individuals pay you for a certification to validate their skills?

   ☐ yes ☐ no

9. Are you a true professional service firm and not a body shop?

   ☐ yes ☐ no

10. Is it clear to a potential buyer that your boutique is not just a well-run lifestyle business?

    ☐ yes ☐ no

If you answered yes to eight or more of these questions, you have a sellable boutique. Your intellectual property will be valued by an acquirer.

If you answered no to eight or more of these questions, you do not have a sellable boutique. There is not enough intellectual property to attract a buyer.

## SUMMARY

There is a lot of confusion as to what intellectual property is. A boutique with true intellectual property is a very valuable boutique. There are many ways to codify knowledge to leverage intellectual property. Lifestyle businesses progress into highly valued boutiques when this intellectual property is created.

## CHAPTER 34

# SALES AND MARKETING PROCESS

Start-ups become boutiques by having the partners generate referrals. Boutiques become market leaders by building a commercial sales engine. Acquirers want to see a maturing commercial capability. The sales and marketing process must prove capable of scaling.

There is an inflection point that all boutiques run into head-on. This is when sales generation happens by the employees and not by the partners. Young prescale firms do not invest in building a professional commercial engine. They do not have to. The partner(s) are experts. They have large personal networks. These personal networks expand as they gain exposure to their niche. The partner(s) harvest these networks for business. Successful projects lead to happy clients. Happy clients lead to positive word of mouth. And positive word of mouth leads to an increase in referrals. More referrals results in more business. This virtuous circle produces enough business for quite a long time. A partner-led sales model can carry a firm through the first five years.

Then it flatlines.

Why?

There are fifty-two weeks in a year, each with five business days. A hardworking partner will put in twelve-hour days. This means that each partner has 3,120 hours to produce. Subtract holidays, a few sick days, and maybe a vacation, and this is more like twenty-five hundred hours. These twenty-five hundred hours are not spent entirely on sales activity. Partners are running the boutique. As the firm scales, partners have about half their time available for business development. These are talented people, which means that each sales hour is fully optimized. There is no waste. Therefore, once each partner is tapped out, sales flatline.

Unless the boutique is prepared to add more partners. Boutiques are reluctant to do this, and I do not blame them. The profit pool is distributed to the partners. Dividing the pie by three is better than dividing the pie by ten. If the sales engine requires more partners, it does not scale. Equity gets diluted.

This is the inflection point. Boutique owners asked themselves to choose between two approaches to sales. Option A is a partner-led model. This means more sales but less wealth for the owners. It requires more partners to scale. Option B is a professional sales model. This means more sales and more wealth for the owners. It does require investment, but it does not eat into the equity. Partners/owners invest budget dollars in hiring a professional sales force. The partners no longer sell. The sales team does the selling.

Acquirers typically want to buy boutiques that have made it through this inflection point. This indicates to them that the boutique can scale. Acquirers are buying the future growth of the boutique. The more likely a boutique is to grow, the more they will want to buy it. Boutiques that can generate sales without the owners' involvement are more likely to grow. Boutiques that take this approach can grow sales cost effectively. A commercial sales team is less expensive than adding partners.

**Boutiques that can generate sales without the owners' involvement are more likely to grow.**

Building a commercial sales team inside a boutique is not easy to do. This is one reason why so few boutiques become market leaders. Failure to pivot away from partner-led sales models results in lifestyle businesses. And potential acquirers are not interested in lifestyle businesses.

Can you prove that you have crossed over this inflection point?

1. Are the owners removed from the sales process?

   ☐ yes ☐ no

2. Are employees generating all the sales?

   ☐ yes ☐ no

3. Is business being generated from scalable sources in addition to referrals?

   ☐ yes ☐ no

4. Have sales increased consistently without adding partners/owners?

   ☐ yes ☐ no

5. Have your financials been able to handle the expense of a commercial sales team?

   ☐ yes ☐ no

6. Have the sales results from the commercial sales team been consistent over time?

   ☐ yes ☐ no

7. Have the win rates with the commercial sales team been on par with the partners'?

   ☐ yes ☐ no

8. Have the deal sizes with the commercial sales team been on par with the partners'?

   ☐ yes ☐ no

9. Have the sales cycle lengths with the commercial sales team been on par with the partners'?

   ☐ yes ☐ no

10. Can the commercial sales team be expanded significantly without breaking the boutique?

    ☐ yes ☐ no

If you answered yes to eight or more of these questions, you have scaled your sales and marketing engine. You will be attractive to an acquirer.

If you answered no to eight or more of these questions, you have yet to scale your sales and marketing engine. You will be less attractive to an acquirer.

## SUMMARY

The path from boutique to market leader results in creating a commercial sales engine. Potential buyers would rather wait until you have made it through this inflection point. Jumping in prior to this is simply too risky for many. If you want to sell your firm, invest resources into developing a scalable sales and marketing engine.

## CHAPTER 35

# EMPLOYEE LOYALTY

Historically, institutional investors have stayed away from investing in professional services firms. They are fond of saying, "All your assets walk out the door each night." This is meant to illustrate that boutiques are asset-light businesses. Assets that leave every day are tough to invest in. Therefore, employee loyalty is mission critical to the selling of your firm.

Boutiques must prove that the assets that leave each night come back in the morning.

Start-ups with ten employees can recover from a 30 percent turnover rate. Hiring three people per year is not an insurmountable task. A boutique with one hundred employees can recover from a 30 percent turnover rate. Hiring thirty people per year is time consuming, but it can be done. A market leader with one thousand employees cannot recover from a 30 percent turnover rate. Hiring three hundred people per year is too hard and costs too much, especially year after year.

Start-ups, boutiques, and market leaders all need to reduce employee turnover. A 30 percent turnover rate means flipping the entire employee base every three years. This puts too great a strain on firms of any size to survive. In professional services, your people are your product. Imagine if Facebook had to rebuild its social network every three years. It just does not work.

Potential acquirers need a gauge of employee loyalty before they write the check.

I recently conducted due diligence on a boutique in the site selection industry. The firm was doing very well, as they specialized in ecommerce warehouse space. The race to same-day delivery capability was creating demand for their services. The location of warehouses can make all the difference for ecommerce fulfillment centers. The site selection decision was complicated, thus driving the need for experts.

**Potential acquirers need a gauge of employee loyalty before they write the check.**

The annual employee turnover was 40 percent and a red flag. My team found and contacted former employees to find out why they quit. They learned that employees were not motivated to stay and succeed. They often cited role corruption, which means that the job was not clearly defined. The star employees did the work of their coworkers. The stars were getting burned out. The millennials wanted to work for a firm with a purpose. And they felt that this boutique had none, other than making the owner rich. It turned out that the annual performance reviews were a joke. They were a compliance-driven exercise. The former employees we spoke to wanted real feedback. One employee mentioned that every time a team member quit, the owner held a pizza party, during which he would run around patting people on the back. This was perceived to be fake, and it turned the employees off. The benefits package placed too much of the burden on the employee. Almost everyone who left the firm landed a job with better pay. The owner was underpaying, and the employees knew it.

Obviously, we did not invest in this firm. I told the owner what we had learned. And I pointed him to resources that can help. I hope that he will address the lack of employee loyalty. If he does, I would be interested investing. But we would need to see improvements in retention, development, and compensation.

At times, boutique owners think that they can hide their skeletons. When you try to sell your firm, interested parties are going to find them. At least, the smart investors will. And my guess is that you do not want to sell your baby to a stupid buyer. This is your life's work.

Assume that every former employee will be contacted during the due diligence process.

Will employee loyalty get in the way of selling your firm?

Ask yourself these questions:

1. Is your turnover rate 15 percent or lower?

   ☐ yes ☐ no

2. Is the average tenure of your employees greater than five years?

   ☐ yes ☐ no

3. Do most of your promotions get filled internally?

   ☐ yes ☐ no

4. Do you have an in-house recruiting engine that provides you with a stream of quality people?

   ☐ yes ☐ no

5. Do you get rewarded by your employees with their discre-

tionary effort?

☐ yes ☐ no

6. Does your boutique have a purpose that the employees believe in?

   ☐ yes ☐ no

7. Does your boutique have a vision of the future that employees want to be a part of?

   ☐ yes ☐ no

8. Does your boutique have a set of values, and are they lived by?

   ☐ yes ☐ no

9. Are you paying your employees what they are worth?

   ☐ yes ☐ no

10. Will your former employees sing your praises when contacted?

    ☐ yes ☐ no

If you answered yes to eight or more of these questions, you have loyal employees. Your boutique will be a reliable investment.

If you answered no to eight or more of these questions, you do not have loyal employees. Your boutique will be a risky investment.

## SUMMARY

You compete in two markets: the market for clients and the market for employees. As much effort needs to be put into employees as into clients. Owners of boutiques work for the employees, not the other way around. Would you want to work for you?

CHAPTER 36

# MANAGEMENT QUALITY

Those who buy boutiques buy management teams first and firms second. The due diligence process is heavily weighted to assess the quality of the management team. It is not cliché to say that our people are our most important asset in the professional services business. Therefore, assessing management quality is of paramount performance.

> **Those who buy boutiques buy management teams first and firms second.**

Acquirers will ask to spend time with the executive leadership plus one. For instance, they will spend time with a partner and with the direct reports of the partner. During these sessions, they will seek to understand the boutique's strategy. And they will determine whether each employee understands their role in it. Strategy, for our purposes here, is where to play and how to win. Investors will look for a crisp, data-supported strategy that identifies both. They will want to see cascading targets that align each employee with the boutique's strategy. The existence of such a strategy would indicate a quality management team.

For example, an architecture boutique in the shopping center market needed to acquire. They had scaled and were now competing for much larger projects. Traditionally they outsourced CAD drafting, for there was not enough work for in-house staff. With the bigger projects, this was no longer true. The owners wanted to bring this in-house to lower costs and improve quality. The time and costs involved with building an in-house CAD drafting studio were unattractive. The buy-versus-build study revealed that it was better to buy. They began looking for a firm to buy. There were several boutiques available. They reached out and got a few interested in the idea. As they spent time with the each, one management team emerged as the best. This team had a tight strategy. The leaders understood the strategy and were able to drive it into the organization. They were able to connect their strategy to the acquiring firm's strategy. It appeared that these two firms would integrate well. This was the boutique that they bought. The other boutiques had similar numbers. On paper they were equal or, in some cases, superior. Yet the boutique that was bought was the one with the best team. Buyers buy teams first and firms second.

The lesson learned from this story is obvious but worth highlighting. The quality of the strategy indicates the quality of the management team.

The management team's vision of the future is equally important to acquirers. For instance, private equity investors are buying the future growth of the boutique. They are going to pay a multiple of today's profits. They need to know that tomorrow's profits will be larger than today's. This is what they are buying. This is how their investment grows. Management teams must prove that the future will be bright. This means explaining the size of the market. Its rate of growth. The share of the market it has and how their share will grow over time. Investors want to know where this growth will come from. Will high water raise all ships? Will the boutique launch new services or enter new markets? Will the growth come from price increases? Will profit growth come from digital transformation? Technology automation? Labor arbitrage? A management team that can articulate a well-thought-out vision is desirable. A compelling vision is an indicator of a quality management team.

The biographies of the management team will also be scrutinized. Do the leaders have the proper level of experience to scale the boutique? Sometimes the team that got you here will not be the team needed going forward. If there are holes in the team, can they be filled? For example, my firm, SBI, operated for years without a human resources leader. With a relatively small number of employees, it was not needed. However, the investors required us to add an HR leader to the team. And we were required to add the cost to the forward projections. This lowered the purchase price, and I pushed back. They explained that we projected hundreds of employees in the future. And this employee base demanded an HR leader. If I wanted to sell, I had to agree to this. The risk of not having an HR leader to the acquirer was too great. We added into the plan the hiring of a HR leader. To complete the sale, I had to plug a hole in our management team. This is not uncommon. A mistake to avoid is an attempt to hide the holes in the management team. This indicates that the management team is of low quality. They are either lying, or worse, they do not recognize the hole.

Will your management team stand up under the scrutiny of due diligence?

1. Is the management team staying with the business postsale?

   ☐ yes ☐ no

2. Is there an industrial-strength strategy developed that an investor can bet on?

   ☐ yes ☐ no

3. Does management quality go at least one layer deep in the organizational chart?

   ☐ yes ☐ no

4. Does the management team drive the strategy deep into the boutique?

   ☐ yes ☐ no

5. Are there cascading targets that reach all the way to the frontline employees?

   ☐ yes ☐ no

6. Is there a believable vision of the future?

   ☐ yes ☐ no

7. Is the management team capable of getting the boutique to this future state?

   ☐ yes ☐ no

8. Is the management team excited and passionate about attempting to do so?

   ☐ yes ☐ no

9. Have all the holes in the team been addressed?

   ☐ yes ☐ no

10. Do the forward projections reflect the true cost to operate the firm in the future?

    ☐ yes ☐ no

If you answered yes to eight or more of these questions, you have an investable team. An acquirer will be satisfied with the quality of the management team.

If you answered no to eight or more of these questions, you do not have an investable management team. An acquirer will not be satisfied with the quality of the team. They are likely to ask you to address the issues prior to investing.

## SUMMARY

Acquirers buy teams first and firms second. The quality of the management team is of major importance to the buyer. It can take years to develop a bankable team. Think like an investor. Would you bet the farm on your team?

## CHAPTER 37

# CULTURE FIT

According to McKinsey, somewhere between one-half and two-thirds of acquisitions fail. They cite as the primary root cause that "organizations overlook cultural issues." *Harvard Business Review* claims that 70 to 90 percent of acquisitions fail and mostly for the same reason. It turns out that culture fit is in the critical path for both buyer and seller.

Boutiques have cultures. Some of them are very strong. These are the ways things get done inside the boutique. It is a common set of beliefs and behaviors. Usually, the culture of the boutique originates from the founder. This entrepreneur designed a firm that they want to work in. Early recruits are those who get along well with the entrepreneur. These early employees perpetuate the culture to the next set of recruits. And on it goes until one day the boutique has hardened around "its" culture. Employees who do not gel with the culture get ejected from it. Like an organ transplant gets rejected from its host. Clients who view the world the way the boutique does become the best clients.

**Clients who view the world the way the boutique does become the best clients.**

Culture fit extends to a certain type of client. Therefore, in professional services firms, deep relationships are formed between boutique and client.

When one firm buys another firm, these two cultures collide. If the core values line up, a smooth integration happens. The two firms become one bigger and better firm. If the core values do not line up, the integration is a mess. The two firms do not become one bigger and better firm. They become separate fiefdoms inside one firm. Turf battles emerge over client ownership, budget, and power structures. Key employees quit. Important clients take their business elsewhere. A lot of effort is expended trying to fix things. This does not work. And the boutiques spin off from each other, taking a different form. The investor is left with a big loss on their scorecard.

How can you determine culture fit before a sale happens?

There are a few things to look for. For example, consider the origin stories. Do the founders have similar backgrounds? Are the founders still a dominant cultural force? Do the early employees resemble the founders? Are they still involved in the business? Have they become legends? If so, what does that tell you about the culture?

Examine the cross-functional collaboration inside the boutique. If there is a lot of it, this portrays a cooperative environment. This would suggest that the boutique is open to help from others. If there is little of it, this suggests a siloed environment. This may indicate a group not open to change and resistant to help.

Look for cultural artifacts. For example, if there are celebrations on significant dates, this would suggest a fun group. If there are contests with leaderboards, this would suggest a competitive group. If employees are acknowledged for years of service, this would suggest a loyal group. If there are a lot of legal documents and rules, this would suggest a cautious group. If there is a relaxed dress code, this would suggest a laid-back group. If people stay at budget inns while traveling, this would suggest a frugal group.

There is no right or wrong culture. The type of culture is not a predictive indicator of success. There are successful boutiques with many different types of culture.

Rather, the question is: "Will our cultures fit?"

The culture at my firm, SBI, was thick. In fact, some new recruits would tell us that you could cut it with a knife. A new employee either took to it immediately or quit inside of a quarter. When we began the process to sell, this was discussed. The partners sticking around after the sale wanted to preserve the culture. Their ideal partner was a passive private equity partner. This meant an investor who left the partners alone. In return, the partners hit the plan. No one wanted MBAs running around with spreadsheets trying to reinvent things. Thankfully, a group of passive investors was interested in SBI. We sold to one of this ilk. The deal avoided failure caused by poor culture fit.

Acquirers are likely to buy boutiques that fit their culture, all else being equal. However, they are likely to pass if there are too many differences.

Can a potential acquirer easily understand your culture?

1. Is the founder still involved in the business?

   ☐ yes ☐ no

2. Does the founder's origin story shed a light on the boutique's culture?

   ☐ yes ☐ no

3. Are the boutique's legends still involved in the business?

   ☐ yes ☐ no

4. Do they personify the boutique's culture?

   ☐ yes ☐ no

5. Does the boutique work well across functions?

   ☐ yes ☐ no

6. Do the artifacts indicate the boutique's culture?

   ☐ yes ☐ no

7. Do employees who are cultural mismatches get rejected by the boutique?

   ☐ yes ☐ no

8. Do the boutique's best clients share a set of common beliefs with the boutique?

   ☐ yes ☐ no

9. Are there deep relationships between the legends and the best clients?

   ☐ yes ☐ no

10. Is it clear to a potential acquirer how your boutique behaves?

    ☐ yes ☐ no

If you answered yes to eight or more of these questions, your sale would not stall during due diligence. Potential acquirers will be clear on who you are. This will allow them to quickly assess fit.

If you answered no to eight or more of these questions, your sale might stall out during due diligence. Potential acquirers know the failure rate of acquisitions. And they understand the critical role that culture fit plays. If they cannot get a take on your culture, they will not proceed.

## SUMMARY

Most acquisitions fail. The primary reason for failure is poor culture fit. Do not hide your culture. Lead with it. You want your sale to be successful. Therefore, you need to find a buyer who fits your culture.

## CHAPTER 38

# ORGANIZATIONAL DESIGN

I have covered organizational design in section 2. My treatment of it there was in the context of it enabling scale. Here in section 3, I will revisit organizational design. The context of this discussion will be enabling a successful exit.

The entity that buys your boutique must figure out the postdeal integration. Difficult integrations are undesirable. They cost a lot, take a long time, and have a high failure rate. Simple integrations are attractive. They are cheap, quick, and have a high success rate.

The design of your boutique's organization can aid, or hurt, the integration. An astute buyer will factor this into their decision-making.

Here is a recent story to illustrate.

One of the world's largest consulting firms was recently trying to acquire. They were looking for a firm to tuck into their digital transformation practice. They serve, among others, the chief marketing officer of large B2B enterprises. And their clients were asking for help with "martech." The slang term *martech* is short for marketing technology. It is the term that the technology marketers use to execute marketing campaigns. The venture capital industry has poured a lot of capital into this niche. This has resulted in a proliferation of tools. Clients need help sorting through these and building their martech stack, as it became known.

This mega firm hired a buy-side investment bank. The bank's team put together a list of potential targets in the martech niche. Calls were made, appointments were set, and pitches took place. During the presentations, the acquirer spent extra time on the organizational design of each boutique. The lead corporate development person kept asking question after question. He explained the organizational model of the large firm he worked for. It was a three-spoke matrix. The first reporting structure was based on geography. The regions had regional headquarters, led by a partner. All the employees in that region rolled into this partner's P&L. The second reporting structure was based on industry. The firm had twenty industry practices, each led by a partner. Employees across geographies also reported to an industry practice. Each industry practice also had a P&L responsibility. The third reporting structure was based on function. The firm had seven functional practices, each led by a partner. Employees across geography and industry also reported to a functional practice. The functional practices also ran separate P&L statements. Each employee had three bosses. It sounds crazy, but this firm has 505,000 employees. A three-tiered matrix is remarkably simple for a firm of this size.

The corporate development person was trying to understand how the boutique would fit. For instance, he would ask each boutique where their headquarters were located. He explored which industries each boutique served. He investigated whether the boutique served the chief marketing officer directly. The reason for this style of inquiry was to determine the postdeal integration. Which partner(s) were going to be responsible for the acquired boutique? How was each practice area's P&L going to be affected? How was the acquisition cost going to be distributed? In particular, he was trying to determine how this would impact partner bonuses. Apparently, partners supported or rejected acquired companies based on bonus impact. If the P&L improved as a result of the deal, so too do the bonuses. In this scenario, merging the boutique is easy. If the P&L deteriorated as a result of the deal, so too did the bonuses. In this scenario, merging the boutique would be difficult.

The acquirer ended up buying a small regional boutique. This boutique could roll easily into the partner's business in that geography. He could absorb the forty-four employees painlessly. In addition, the boutique's revenue was mostly from one industry. This made it simple to assign dual responsibility to that industry's partner. The investment bank was surprised at the outcome. They were hoping that the large firm, his client, bought a larger boutique. Their fee was tied to deal size. However, the client chose a small boutique because their organizational model was simple to absorb. This meant an easy integration, which meant a successful acquisition.

The lesson to take from this story is straightforward. The easier your organizational model is to digest, the likelier you are to be bought. At times, boutiques unnecessarily complicate their organizational models. This will make it hard to sell your firm. As a rule, organize around geography, industry, or function. Stay away from a matrix. Stay small enough to be able to sell. Acquirers tend to shy away from buying boutiques with

**The easier your organizational model is to digest, the likelier you are to be bought.**

hundreds of employees. They are tough to integrate. This, of course, is if you are selling to a strategic partner. If you are selling to a financial buyer, this is less of an issue. They are less concerned with organizational model and more concerned with EBITDA.

Is your organizational model conducive to a sale?

Let us find out.

1. Will your organizational model be easy to absorb?

   ☐ yes ☐ no

2. Are you organized around either geography, industry, or function?

   ☐ yes ☐ no

3. Have you steered clear of the matrix?

   ☐ yes ☐ no

4. Are you large enough to be interesting but small enough to integrate easily?

   ☐ yes ☐ no

5. Does your organizational model reflect the niche you serve?

   ☐ yes ☐ no

6. Does your organizational model reflect your business model?

   ☐ yes ☐ no

7. Is the organizational model a good starting point for an easy integration?

   ☐ yes ☐ no

8. Is your organizational model flexible enough to morph into somebody else's?

   ☐ yes ☐ no

9. Does the organizational model reflect the true cost to operate your boutique?

   ☐ yes ☐ no

10. Will it be obvious to a potential acquirer where the synergies will come from?

   ☐ yes ☐ no

If you answered yes to eight or more of these questions, your organizational model would attract buyers.

If you answered no to eight or more of these questions, your organizational model would discourage buyers.

## SUMMARY

The perceived difficulty, or ease, of integrating your boutique will affect your sale. Understand the organizational model of the type of firms that might buy you. Redesign your model to be seamlessly integrated if bought. This will increase the chances of exiting.

CHAPTER 39

# CONTINUOUS IMPROVEMENT

The last thing market leaders want when buying a boutique is a development project. They want a boutique that hits the ground running. A boutique that is accretive immediately. Therefore, during due diligence, they will seek to understand your continuous improvement process.

How will they do this?

There are several ways.

Acquirers will look to see how, and how often, methodologies are updated. They do not want boutiques with aging methods that are no longer attractive to clients. For instance, a management consulting firm specializing in Six Sigma was hot in the 1990s. But not so much today. Boutiques that are relying on aging cash cows have good financials now. However, these financials will not be good tomorrow. Unless the boutique can continuously improve.

Buyers will also look to see how modern the engagement models are. For example, the world changed during COVID-19. Clients are now comfortable with boutiques serving them virtually. Boutiques that still require their employees to camp out on-site are antiquated. Outdated engagement models suggest a firm struggling to continuously improve.

Potential buyers will establish historical client satisfaction trend lines. And they will project these into the future. If a boutique's client satisfaction has hovered in the low eighties for a decade, continuous improvement is nonexistent.

Technology adoption is a sign of continuous improvement. If a boutique is still producing decks as deliverables, this is a bad sign. Today there is an app for everything. Decks as deliverables suggest that the boutique has not evolved its tech capability. In a shop like this, you will often hear, "This is how we have always done it."

Profits are another sign of continuous improvement. To increase profits, a boutique needs to decouple revenue from head-count growth. This is the essence of scale. A boutique whose revenue growth and head-count growth are the same is not continuously improving.

Pricing is an excellent indicator of continuous improvement. If a boutique can raise the prices of its existing clients, it is continuously improving. The same client willing to pay more for the same service is a great sign. This says that the quality of the work has gone up. And the client has validated the improved quality by paying more for it. Profit increases from existing clients suggest an improving firm.

**The best clients hire the boutique because it says something about them when they do. Client quality is the purest sign of continuous improvement.**

The ultimate sign of continuous improvement is the boutique's client roster. For instance, three years ago a boutique attracted struggling clients. These struggling clients hired the boutique because the prestigious firms would not work with them. Today the boutique's clients are household brand names. The best clients hire the boutique because it says something about them when they do. Client quality is the purest sign of continuous improvement.

Can you prove that you improve continuously?

1. Do you version control your methodologies?

   ☐ yes ☐ no

2. Do you progressively certify your employees?

   ☐ yes ☐ no

3. Are you charging existing clients more for the same service?

   ☐ yes ☐ no

4. Are your client satisfaction scores trending up over time?

   ☐ yes ☐ no

5. Are your employee engagement scores trending up over time?

   ☐ yes ☐ no

6. Are your profit margins trending up over time?

   ☐ yes ☐ no

7. Have your engagement models moved from on-site to virtual, at least partially?

   ☐ yes ☐ no

8. Have client deliverables been digitized?

   ☐ yes ☐ no

9. Have your price levels trended up over time?

   ☐ yes ☐ no

10. Has the quality of your client roster improved over time?

☐ yes ☐ no

If you answered yes to eight or more of these questions, you are continuously improving.

If you answered no to eight or more of these questions, you are a fix-it project. Potential acquirers will not be attracted to you.

## SUMMARY

What have you done for me lately? Buyers of your boutique are purchasing who you are becoming. They are not buying who you have been. Yesterday is worthless to them. They are looking forward. They need to be excited about your potential to improve.

# CHAPTER 40
# INNOVATION

Innovation is a new idea. A new service. A new business model. Boutiques that innovate grow and scale rapidly. They, more than the continuous improvers, become the market leaders.

**Boutiques that innovate grow and scale rapidly.**

There are many great examples of innovation in the professional services industry. For example, in the 1960s, Boston Consulting Group (BCG) exploded onto the scene. Their leader, Bruce Henderson, invented the experience curve. This proved that a company's costs fell as their experience increased. Today this is widely understood, but back then this was a real innovation. BCG became a market leader and now employs over fifteen thousand people.

In the 1920s, the recorded deposition changed the litigator's relationship to witness testimony forever. Law firms that were early to adopt this practice thrived. Today it is impossible to imagine the law without recorded depositions.

Where would the accounting industry be without the Italian

Luca Bartolomes Pacioli? Around 1500, he invented a system of record keeping that used a ledger. Later, he wrote the first accounting books explaining the use of journals. This earned him the title of "the father of bookkeeping."

And how about N. W. Ayer? In the nineteenth century, he founded the first full-service advertising agency. Rather than just selling space, he offered planning, creative, and campaign execution. He became famous for serving De Beers, AT&T, and the US Army. Have you ever heard the slogan "When it rains, it pours"? Or "A diamond is forever"? This is the firm that created these iconic mottoes.

Today our industry is filled with groundbreakers. These pioneers are inspiring.

In 2008, the distributed ledger, a.k.a. blockchain, was invented by Satoshi Nakamoto. Transactions will never be the same. Interestingly, this name is thought to be an alias. No one knows for sure who invented the distributed ledger.

Have you ever heard of Daniel Kuenzi? He is an architect who turned shipping containers into modular farms. He can grow the equivalent yield of five conventional outdoor farms in one shipping container.

Check out the web design firm Wix. They are injecting artificial intelligence into web design. A client inputs content and preferences, and the tool pops out a website in no time at all. They get to a template in a nanosecond by mining lessons learned from scanning examples.

You get the point. The professional services industry has been innovating for centuries. And it continues to innovate.

Investors are looking for upside. They will value your firm on the current results. However, they may go with you over someone else if you are an innovator. Who knows, maybe you or a teammate will invest something that alters the future?

The wow factor matters.

Are you an innovator?

1. Have you pioneered a new approach in your niche?

   ☐ yes ☐ no
2. Are you more than a one-hit wonder?

   ☐ yes ☐ no
3. Has your industry adopted your way of doing things?

   ☐ yes ☐ no
4. Does your industry use your language as its own?

   ☐ yes ☐ no
5. Do the smartest in your niche come to you with the most challenging issues?

   ☐ yes ☐ no
6. Has an ecosystem of boutiques formed around your innovation?

   ☐ yes ☐ no
7. Do you mainstage the keynote for the most important industry conference?

   ☐ yes ☐ no
8. Do you get more than $50,000 for a speech?

   ☐ yes ☐ no
9. Do employees join your firm for the opportunity to work next to you?

   ☐ yes ☐ no
10. Have you created a legacy that will live on in your niche after you leave?

    ☐ yes ☐ no

If you answered yes to eight or more of these questions, you are an innovator.

If you answered no to eight or more of these questions, you are not an innovator.

## SUMMARY

The wow factor matters. Like it or not, you are in show business. You are an expert. And your firm is made up of experts. No one wants to buy the boutique that regurgitates other people's innovations. They want to buy the songwriters, a.k.a. the Rolling Stones.

CHAPTER 41

# FINANCIAL MARKET TRENDS

The ability to sell your firm will be impacted by the environment. There is a good time to sell and a not so good time to sell. And this has nothing to do with your firm. The financial market trends can put the wind at your back or in your face.

For instance, the level of deal activity in your niche matters. Niches get hot, and they go cold. At times, investors suffer from herd mentality. If they see a lot of boutiques like yours trading, they want to play. Investment capital is like a moth to a flame.

It is important for you to know the drivers behind the deal activity. What are the reasons boutiques like yours are getting bought right now? A little while back, data science boutiques got gobbled up left and right. The driver behind the activity was a shortage of data scientists. Large companies were funding big data projects. Their consumers moved online and began generating huge amounts of data. Companies needed to understand this data to better understand their customers. They did not have the talent in-house, so they turned to boutiques and market leaders. The demand was big, and it was now. The large firms did not have the time to build out slowly. They went into the market and began buying data science boutiques. This was the driver behind the deal activity.

What is yours?

Economic cycles matter as well. During times of expansion, there is a lot of deal activity. Large firms are trying to grow, and acquisitions are part of it. Cash flow is up, so there is investment capital to do deals. Private equity investors can raise a great deal of capital during the good times. They need to deploy it. As such, they go on a buying spree. In contrast, during recessionary times, deal activity falls. Fewer boutiques want to go to market when their financials do not look great. Market leaders and private equity investors become cautious and pull in the reins a bit.

Multiyear industry trends can help or hurt. Healthy organic growth rates for your industry over a decade help a lot. Investors want exposure to growing markets. Success can be had without a bloody share battle. In contrast, industries in decline are not the place to be. No one ever got rich being the best of a bad bunch.

Debt markets play a big role. How a company pays for your boutique determines the return. If they must pay for your boutique with cash, it is a harder sell. Why? There are other priorities competing for that cash. For instance, maybe it is better to do a share buyback. If the banks are lending, this makes it an easier sell. If your boutique can service the debt. Unfortunately, banks are reluctant to lend to boutiques and to those buying boutiques. Boutiques are labeled as asset-light businesses. This is code for there is not enough collateral to secure the

**No one ever got rich being the best of a bad bunch.**

loans. However, into this void are private lending institutions. They charge a higher rate but are willing to lend to boutiques. All this is to say that the health of the debt markets impacts your sale. Be sure to understand debt financing.

The right time to sell is when there are large pools of available capital. The wrong time to sell is when money is tight.

Are there large pools of available capital in your niche?

Spend some time investigating this. Timing matters.

Are the financial market trends in your favor right now?

1. Are there large pools of available capital in your niche?

   ☐ yes ☐ no

2. Are the multiyear industry trends of your niche favorable?

   ☐ yes ☐ no

3. Are banks lending in your niche?

   ☐ yes ☐ no

4. Are private lending institutions interested in your niche?

   ☐ yes ☐ no

5. Are the interest rates attractive?

   ☐ yes ☐ no

6. Can your boutique handle a decent amount of debt on the balance sheet?

   ☐ yes ☐ no

7. Are deals happening in your space?

   ☐ yes ☐ no

8. Do you know the drivers of this deal activity?

   ☐ yes ☐ no

9. Are you at the right point in the economic cycle?

   ☐ yes ☐ no

10. If they had to, would a buyer make you an all-cash offer?

    ☐ yes ☐ no

If you answered yes to eight or more of these questions, you have favorable financial markets at your service.

If you answered no to eight or more of these questions, you have some headwinds. It may not be the right time to sell.

## SUMMARY

There is a good time to sell. And there is a bad time to sell. Unfortunately, this is largely out of your control. Focus on building a highly desirable boutique and be patient. Wait for the sun to be shining.

CHAPTER 42

# COMPARABLES

The value of your boutique is influenced by your comps. What are comps? Comps is short for the word *comparables*. These are the valuations, and terms, for boutiques like yours that recently sold.

Boutique comps are analogous to home sale comps. Think of the last time you sold a home. You hired a real estate agent. They pulled a list of homes that recently sold in your neighborhood. They calculated a price per square foot from these comparables. They then applied this price per square foot to your home and recommended a price.

In this sense, investment bankers are like real estate agents. Instead of selling homes, they sell companies. They pull a list of boutiques that recently sold in your category. The category can be thought of as the neighborhood. They find out the price paid for the boutique. This is expressed as a multiple of EBITDA. The multiple of EBITDA can be thought of as the price per square foot in this analogy. They apply this EBITDA multiple to your boutique and recommend a price.

The value of your home might go up or down slightly. For

example, if you recently updated the kitchen, you get a higher price per square foot. Or if the home needs a roof, you might sell for a lower price per square foot. The value of your boutique might go up or down similarly. For instance, if you are growing 30 percent, your multiple of EBITDA might be higher. Or if your revenue is flat, your multiple of EBITDA might be lower.

The lesson from this is to ensure that your comps are accurate. You would not want your house to be compared to an apartment. And you would not want your boutique to be placed in the wrong category.

My firm, SBI, was originally placed in the sales training category. This was not correct. We did not train sales teams. We were a management consulting firm specializing in sales effectiveness. The correct comps for us were other management consulting firms. This impacted the multiple of EBITDA greatly. At the time, sales training firms traded at five and a half times EBITDA. Management consulting firms traded at nine times EBITDA. In addition, sales training firms were not perceived to be high growth. Yet we had a ten-year compounded annual growth rate of 30 percent. When correctly placed in the high-growth category, our multiple went from nine times to eleven times.

The two changes in comps doubled the EBITDA multiple paid for my boutique. This resulted in tens of millions more in wealth creation.

Get your comps right.

The price paid for your boutique is one side of a two-sided coin. The other side is the terms of the deal. Comparables affect the terms as well. Let me return to the house analogy to explain. If the home buyer pays cash, that is a specific deal term. If the seller pays the closing costs, that is a specific deal term. If the closing date is ninety days from today, that is a deal term.

Boutiques, like homes, have terms to govern their deals. For example, if the deal involved a three-year earn-out, that is a deal term. If the seller agrees to a three-year noncompete, that is a deal term. If the representations and warranty period is eighteen months, that is a deal term.

Sometimes deal terms can be more important than the price. In my case, I required to be paid in full up front with no earn-out. I also was unwilling to roll over any of my equity. And I was not interested in staying employed during a transition period. These were my terms. My terms were unacceptable to some investors. When they heard them, they decided not to bid. Some investors agreed to these terms, and, of course, one investor won the bid.

**Sometimes deal terms can be more important than the price.**

As investors considered my terms, they referenced the comps. And this steered my boutique into a category of buyer. The large management consulting firms had a long history of buying boutiques. Most had never done a deal with these terms. Their comps told them to walk away. The strategics, as they are known, took a pass. The private equity firms also had a long history of buying boutiques. Most had never done a deal with my terms. Their comps told them to walk away. They had a real problem with the rejection of the equity rollover. My boutique was not for them. However, the investors who fund management buyouts had done many deals like this. Their comps told them that these were standard terms, and they did the deal.

The lesson from the flip side of the coin is to know your buyer type. Certain buyers require certain deal terms. This is often based on the deals they typically do. The comps, as we call them. Pursue the buyers whose deal terms align with your reasons for selling. Trying to sell your boutique in a way that is foreign to your buyer is almost impossible. It is hard enough to exit. You do not need to make it harder with the square-peg-in-the-round-hole approach.

Do you understand your comps?

1. Do you have a list of boutiques in your category that recently sold?

   ☐ yes ☐ no
2. Do you know the price paid for each?

   ☐ yes ☐ no
3. Do you know the deal terms for each?

   ☐ yes ☐ no
4. Do you know the investment banker who represented each?

   ☐ yes ☐ no
5. Do you know the names of the investors who bid on each?

   ☐ yes ☐ no
6. Do you know who won the big for each?

   ☐ yes ☐ no
7. Do you know exactly why the winner won?

   ☐ yes ☐ no
8. Is your boutique in the correct category?

   ☐ yes ☐ no
9. Is the correct category for your boutique obvious to potential buyers?

   ☐ yes ☐ no

10. Are you trying to sell your boutique to the right group of buyers?

    ☐ yes ☐ no

If you answered yes to eight or more of these questions, you have increased your odds of success.

If you answered no to eight or more of these questions, you might get taken advantage of.

## SUMMARY

Comparables are important. They can add to or subtract from the purchase price. They can be the difference between acceptable or unacceptable terms. Be sure that you are in the correct category. And be sure to pursue the correct buyer group.

## CHAPTER 43

# UNIVERSE OF BUYERS

Supply and demand will impact your ability to sell your boutique. Consider the supply side part of the equation. If there are many boutiques like yours available for sale, the price goes down. If you are the only one available, the price goes up. The same can be said on the demand side. If the universe of buyers is wide and deep, the chances of a successful exit increase. If the number of potential buyers is small, an exit will be hard.

This is where the investment banker earns their fee. It is their job to develop a large universe of potential buyers. How do they do this?

The banker will work with you to build a market map. This highlights all the firms in your space that might be candidates. It also highlights the firms in the adjacent market segments. These are firms that are not in your space but that might want to be. They are often in markets adjacent to yours. Be sure to build an exhaustive list.

The banker will add to this market map the active private equity firms in your segment. These are investors the banker knows are looking for deals like yours. Again, be sure to build an exhaustive list.

Before the banker reaches out to potential buyers, you need to prepare them. You do this by giving them a compelling strategic rationale to buy your boutique. This is not the time to be efficient. This is the time to be effective. Develop a custom rationale for each possible buyer. Think as a potential buyer might think.

**Develop a custom rationale for each possible buyer. Think as a potential buyer might think.**

For example, maybe buying your boutique opens a new market. Or maybe it strengthens the potential buyer's value proposition. Maybe it makes them better equipped to compete with a set of rivals. Or, at times, it can diversify a revenue stream. Sometimes it solves a client concentration issue. Can buying your boutique help the buyer raise their prices? There are many possibilities. The banker needs to articulate a crisp strategic rationale to buy your boutique. And the banker is not you. They are not going to know what you know. It is your job to make them successful. Arm them with the story.

A registered investment adviser (RIA) recently bought a bookkeeping boutique. On paper, this is an odd couple. An RIA is a boutique that advises high net worth individuals on investments. They manage investment portfolios. They are registered with the Securities and Exchange Commission. RIAs charge high fees for complex work.

A bookkeeping firm does none of the above. They generally do data entry into accounting ledgers. They are focused on recording a business's financial transactions. This involves maintaining records, tracking transactions, and paying bills. Bookkeeping boutiques charge low fees for commodity work.

The owner of the bookkeeping firm got sick. Fortunately, he battled cancer and won. But this experience changed his outlook on life. He wanted to retire, and to do so, he needed to sell his boutique. He hired a creative investment banker to represent his boutique. The owner provided a list of the large bookkeeping services to the banker's team. He assumed that the big firms would want to buy his business. This was the customary way that boutiques like his exited. The banker's team poured through his financials. They noticed that some of the top clients were RIAs. The team called the bookkeeping boutique's clients. They wanted to learn why these RIAs were great loyal customers. The findings were surprising. It turned out that the RIA field had gotten very crowded. The increased competition required these RIAs to offer more value. They started handling tax preparation. This morphed into taking on the client's bookkeeping. RIAs learned that if you did a client's books, they did not defect. And client retention in this business is a strategic imperative.

The bankers proceeded to build a list of RIAs. They hired a call center firm to call into each RIA on the list. The goal was to determine which did not offer bookkeeping services yet. This produced a list of target RIAs to reach out to. The calls went out. The bank team started communicating the strategic rationale of an RIA offering bookkeeping services. The reduction in client attrition was very compelling. A group of RIAs got it, and they were offered a chance to bid. A bidding war unfolded, and our cancer survivor road off into the sunset. He exited successfully.

This is an example of building a universe of buyers. Sometimes the potential buyers are not obvious.

The interesting part of this story is the outreach. If the owner of the bookkeeping service reached out directly, he would have failed. He would not have been credible. He would have appeared as some weird guy trying to sell his firm. However, the investment bank had credibility. The RIAs know an investment bank is selective as to who they represent. They work on commission. They do not want to represent a weak boutique. They are hard to sell. The banker's reputation enabled the calls to be returned. And it was the banker who got the RIAs engaged in the bidding process.

The lesson to learn here is to hire an investment banker. Be sure to hire the right one. You get what you pay for. You might not be taken seriously without proper representation.

Do you have a wide and deep universe of potential buyers?

1. Do you know how many firms like yours are for sale?

   ☐ yes ☐ no

2. Have you completed a market map?

   ☐ yes ☐ no

3. Has this map produced an exhaustive list of potential buyers?

   ☐ yes ☐ no

4. Has this map produced an exhaustive list of potential buyers from adjacent markets?

   ☐ yes ☐ no

5. Has this list been augmented with private equity firms with a known interest in boutiques like yours?

   ☐ yes ☐ no

6. Have you developed a compelling strategic rationale to buy your boutique?

   ☐ yes ☐ no

7. Has this strategic rationale been customized for each potential buyer?

   ☐ yes ☐ no

8. Do you know who the leading investment bank is in your niche?

   ☐ yes ☐ no

9. Have you approached them about representing your boutique?

   ☐ yes ☐ no

10. Has the investment bank creatively enlarged the universe of potential buyers?

    ☐ yes ☐ no

If you answered yes to eight or more of these questions, you have a large universe of potential buyers.

If you answered no to eight or more of these questions, your buyer universe is not wide or deep enough.

## SUMMARY

Supply and demand will impact your exit. Take the time to strategically approach the market. The goal is to build a wide and deep universe of potential buyers. There are more buyers than you realize. Many of whom would like to hear your compelling rationale for a deal.

## CHAPTER 44

# DE-RISK

Investors' default position is to find reasons not to buy your boutique. They approach due diligence trying to find ways to de-risk their investment. Committing the capital and the time to your deal is a high-stakes bet. Can you make it smoothly through due diligence?

A few years ago, a media-buying agency put itself up for sale. In simple terms, they bought space from media companies and sold it to advertising agencies. Their specialty was newspapers. It sounds crazy today, but back then this was big business. Newspapers generated most of their revenue from advertising. Advertising agencies had clients who wanted to run their ads in these newspapers. A broker, called a media representative, often sat in the middle. The broker would buy the space from the newspaper and resell to the advertising agencies. This was the business of this boutique. And before the internet reshaped the advertising industry, this boutique thrived. As did many of them.

A roll up of media representative firms was happening. A few large firms were purchasing the boutiques. There was a lot of interest in this boutique. However, a deal never got done, and this owner eventually filed bankruptcy.

What went wrong?

The owner was unable to complete the due diligence process quickly. His financials were a mess because his personal life was wrapped up in them. He tried to increase the reported profits with dozens of add backs. An add back is when an expense is added back to the profits of a business. He had family members on the payroll who did not work at the boutique. His salary did not reflect the true cost of the position in the open market. He was charging family vacations to the boutique as business expenses. The list goes on. With much effort, this all could have been sorted out. However, the acquirers were in a land grab. They did not have the time to clear the fog around this boutique. And they did not have to. There were many boutiques like this one available for sale. And the process with them was simple and straightforward. The effort needed for this boutique was not worth it.

This owner lost out because he got to cute with his taxes. The financial mess was caused by an owner trying to save a few tax bucks. In this case, the cliché penny wise and pound foolish is accurate.

Owners of boutiques are often entrepreneurs. This is to say that they are risk-takers. And in many ways, this is the reason they are successful. However, risk-taking and carelessness are not the same thing. It is careless to get cute with your taxes. Aggressive accounting practices do not make your boutique attractive. Nor does it pay to be careless with the law. Nothing scares a buyer away faster than a pending lawsuit. Do yourself a favor and stay clear of regulators. Acquirers do not want the risk associated with regulatory

**Nothing scares a buyer away faster than a pending lawsuit.**

violations.

Will you be able to make it through due diligence smoothly and quickly?

1. Do you have five years of audited financials?

   ☐ yes ☐ no

2. Do you have five years of tax returns?

   ☐ yes ☐ no

3. Are you operating according to industry-standard accounting principles?

   ☐ yes ☐ no

4. Do you have few, if any, add backs?

   ☐ yes ☐ no

5. Is your personal financial life clearly separated from the business financials?

   ☐ yes ☐ no

6. Have you never been sued?

   ☐ yes ☐ no

7. Have you never sued anyone?

   ☐ yes ☐ no

8. Are you clear of any outstanding legal action?

   ☐ yes ☐ no

9. Are you using industry-standard legal contracts with clients, employees, and suppliers?

   ☐ yes ☐ no

10. Are you compliant with industry regulations?

    ☐ yes ☐ no

If you answered yes to eight or more of these questions, you will be easy to acquire.

If you answered no to eight or more of these questions, you may be too much work to buy.

## SUMMARY

Do not give a buyer a reason to say no. Run a tight ship. Run your boutique by the book. Operating in the gray area will make a potential buyer nervous. Any gain from doing so is just not worth it.

# CHAPTER 45
# BUY VERSUS BUILD

Strategic acquirers start with a fundamental question: "Should we buy this boutique or build the practice internally?" To sell your boutique, it must be more attractive for a strategic to buy.

What makes it more attractive to buy?

Time, cost, and probability of success.

Strategics are usually filling a gap. The market shifts, and at times, the market leader's service portfolio is lacking. This gap can be filled by building a practice internally. And it can be filled through an acquisition.

The urgency on which this gap needs to be filled is key. If the market allows for the strategic to build, they will. If the market is moving fast, the strategic will buy. For instance, market leader Accenture made several acquisitions in cybersecurity in 2018–2019. Cybersecurity is a top agenda item in boardrooms. There is an arms race going on between the hackers and the companies. The cost of a breach is so high that firms cannot take the time to build. The urgency of the gap influenced Accenture to buy.

Time is not the only variable in the analysis. Cost is equally important. For example, marketing agencies have been buying IT service providers. Marketing has been, and will continue to be, more digital. It is expensive for marketing agencies to build out IT service capabilities. Those who have attempted this have made a lot of mistakes. And paid a lot of dumb taxes. It is most cost effective to acquire boutiques with specific digital capabilities.

Probability of success is often added to time and cost when deciding to buy or build. Professional services firms are only as successful as their reputations allow. A few high-profile failed projects, and a firm could become worthless. For instance, back in 2014, MillerCoors was running seven different instances of SAP. This was the result of years of acquisitions. Each acquired company came with its own instance. They hired Indian IT services firm HCL Technologies to unify into one system. The project went so poorly that MillerCoors sued for $100 million in 2017. HCL Technologies countersued, and the two sides eventually worked it out. However, this story lives on forever online. This makes it more difficult for the service provider to win new clients. Strategics want and need to go after big projects with big brand-name clients. However, they do not want high-profile failures. Therefore, they will often buy boutiques to shore up any gaps in capabilities.

**Professional services firms are only as successful as their reputations allow.**

SBI was sold to a private equity firm due in part to this buy-versus-build dynamic. Early in the process, many strategic buyers expressed interest. However, we were growing quickly, which drove up the price. The strategic buyers did the math on a per head basis. They calculated that they could build their sales practice for less than buying us. These strategic buyers also felt that the internal build was less risky than an external buy. SBI would get them there faster.

However, for some, speed was not enough to overcome risk and cost. In contrast, the private equity buyers did not care about buy versus build. They were investors and would never contemplate building a sales consulting practice. The buy-versus-build decision made us more attractive to private equity investors and less attractive to strategic buyers.

On the dimensions of time, cost, and probability of success, how do you score? Think this through for each of your possible strategic acquirers. Can they easily replicate what you do? Can they do it quickly? Can they do it for less than what it will cost to buy you?

A compelling buy-versus-build story for each strategic is your best friend.

Use these questions to help develop the story:

1. Has the market shifted, creating a gap in the service portfolios of your market leaders?

   ☐ yes ☐ no

2. Are the market leaders you compete with aware of the gap?

   ☐ yes ☐ no

3. Is the gap urgent?

   ☐ yes ☐ no

4. Have you directly competed with a market leader on a deal in this specific gap area?

   ☐ yes ☐ no

5. Did you win?

   ☐ yes ☐ no

6. Does the market leader know they lost to you?

   ☐ yes ☐ no

7. Do they know they lost because you have a capabilities advantage over them?

   ☐ yes ☐ no

8. If they were to fill the gap, would it be fastest to buy you?

   ☐ yes ☐ no

9. If they were to fill the gap, would it be cheaper to buy you than to build internally?

   ☐ yes ☐ no

10. Are the chances of successfully filling the gap better if they buy you?

    ☐ yes ☐ no

If you answered yes to eight or more of these questions, strategics will find you extremely attractive. It is in their best interests to buy.

If you answered no to eight or more of these questions, strategics will find you unattractive. It is in their best interests to build internally.

## SUMMARY

The buy-versus-build discussion is happening. With or without you. It is best for you to participate in that discussion. Make a strong case that buying you is faster, cheaper, and more successful.

CHAPTER 46

# SHAREHOLDER AND STAKEHOLDER ALIGNMENT

A common reason that attempts to exit fail is a lack of shareholder alignment. A good deal for some shareholders is not a good deal for others. Disagreements over who gets what, and when they get it, have sunk many deals. Greed is a powerful force. The same is true when stakeholder alignment is lacking. Stakeholders generally like the way it is and do not want things to change. They often try to prevent a deal from happening and can get in the way.

It is important to have a definition of the term *shareholder* and to understand how it is different from the term *stakeholder*. Boutique owners must have alignment with both when selling.

A shareholder is anyone who owns a share in the boutique. Most boutiques are set up as private partnerships. This typically means that there is more than one shareholder. The partners each own shares in the firm. At times, there are additional shareholders. For instance, it is not uncommon to find friends and family owning shares. They provide start-up capital to get the boutique off the ground, and they own shares as a result.

Shareholders have certain rights, such as voting on distributions and/or selling the boutique. These rights are protected by legal agreements. Selling your boutique often requires their agreement.

A stakeholder is a person or a group that has a stake in the business. For instance, your bank is a stakeholder and so is your landlord. Your key employees and clients are stakeholders. These groups depend on you in some way. Your bank depends on you to make your loan payments. Your landlord needs you to pay the rent. Your key employees depend on you for their paychecks.

Stakeholders have certain rights as well. Some of these rights are explicit and protected by contracts. Examples are lease agreements, loan agreements, and the like. Some of these rights are implied and are not protected by contracts. Examples are employee retention, repeat business from clients, and so on. However, the stakeholder rights that are technically not protected may as well be. For instance, a key client who does not support your deal can kill it with one phone call.

**To close your deal, your shareholders and stakeholders will have to say yes.**

To close your deal, your shareholders and stakeholders will have to say yes. If they say no, they can hold up your exit.

Allow me to share a story. An owner of a boutique wanted to sell his marketing automation practice. He was an early entrant in the fast-growing niche and did well. However, the field was getting crowded. There were dozens of competitors now. The software companies he partnered with were being consolidated. SalesForce.com bought Exact Target. Adobe bought Marketo. Oracle bought Eloqua. His relationships were with the executives in the companies getting bought. They provided him with a stream of leads. They were all leaving within a year or two of selling their firms. Their replacements were strangers who preferred to distribute leads to a broader base of service partners. It was time to get out.

The owner's banker did an excellent job. He got the boutique a compelling offer. The owner stood to exit with a lot of money and on favorable terms. However, the shareholders were upset. He had allowed a few key employees to buy into his firm over the years. They each held a small stake, but collectively, it added up. The acquirer required these key employees to stay on postsale. Included in the deal package was employment contracts for the team. This specified their titles, responsibilities, reporting structure, compensation, and stock option plan. It required each key employee to sign a three-year restricted covenant agreement. This included some sticky items, such as noncompete and no solicitation clauses. The employees refused to sign. They decided to hold the owner hostage. This group issued some demands in exchange for signing the employment agreements. The owner, feeling betrayed, dug in and refused to meet their demands. He felt that he was being extorted and that the demands were not reasonable: inflated salaries, huge retention bonuses, accelerated vesting schedules. The acquirer did not like what they saw and backed out of the deal. They felt that they themselves might get bought down the road, and they did not want this group in their company. They might try the same feet-to-the-fire negotiation tactics with them.

The investment banker was very experienced. He was keeping the runner-up warm while this played out. This potential acquirer was willing to step in and do a deal. The banker went to the key employees and got their buy-in. He did this prior to revealing the new deal terms. He explained to this group how fragile the situation was. They understood that they blew the last deal. And this was grounds for termination. The owner, unlikely to sell now, was going to replace each one of them. And rightfully so. The remedy to this mess was a new deal with a new buyer. The key employees, seeing that this was the best path, expressed their minimum requirements, which were in line with the new acquirers' expectations. After a few weeks of drama, the deal closed. Everyone got what they wanted.

The lesson to learn here is that alignment must be in place. Human nature is a tricky thing. You never know how people are going to behave under stress. Shareholders and stakeholders can, and will, act unpredictably. It is wise to get everyone in alignment prior to trying to sell. And long before an offer is submitted.

Are your shareholders and stakeholders aligned?

1. Do you have more than one shareholder?

   ☐ yes ☐ no

2. Do they agree on an acceptable price?

   ☐ yes ☐ no

3. Do they agree on the terms of a deal?

   ☐ yes ☐ no

4. Are their expectations realistic?

   ☐ yes ☐ no

5. Do you have multiple stakeholder groups?

   ☐ yes ☐ no

6. Do you know what each stakeholder group wants?

   ☐ yes ☐ no

7. Are their expectations realistic?

   ☐ yes ☐ no

8. Do you know which stakeholder groups can get in the way of your sale?

   ☐ yes ☐ no

9. Do you know what the acquirer will require from each?

   ☐ yes ☐ no

10. Can you find a compromise between the acquirer and the stakeholder group?

    ☐ yes ☐ no

If you answered yes to eight or more of these questions, your shareholders and stakeholders are aligned.

If you answered no to eight or more of these questions, your shareholders and stakeholders may hold up the sale.

## SUMMARY

Shareholders own part of your firm. They have rights and will need to agree with your deal. You also have key stakeholder groups. They also will need to agree for you to close. It is best to get into alignment prior to trying to sell. There is usually a compromise that makes everyone happy. However, this compromise can be hard to locate under the hot lights of a deal.

# CHAPTER 47
# SUSTAINABILITY OF PERFORMANCE

The number one reason that exits fail is a decline in performance during the sales process. Going into the sales process, you must ensure that you can sustain performance.

How?

There are a few best practices to follow.

**The number one reason that exits fail is a decline in performance during the sales process.**

First, time the sales process to a robust backlog. My suggestion is to have at least nine months of work under contract. For example, let us say that your forward twelve-month revenue projection is $50 million. Nine months, or $37.5 million, should be under contract before you begin the process. A sales process will take nine to twelve months. A nine-month backlog will keep the cash flowing in at a crucial time.

Second, time the sales process to a strong pipeline. I suggest a

5:1 project pipeline. For example, let us say that your twelve-month projections for new projects is $10 million. This suggests having visibility on $50 million in new projects before the process begins. A 5:1 project pipeline provides enough coverage to hit the target.

Third, divide the business development team in two. The first team is committed to generating new business. The second team is committed to selling the boutique. A mistake to avoid is to underestimate the sales work in selling the firm. For example, owners are typically rainmakers. They bring in a lot of new business for the boutique. When their time is consumed with selling the firm, they are not bringing in new business. The revenue takes a hit and the exit falls apart. Be sure to account for the owner being consumed with the exit. Reassign this work to other capable partners. Keep the new business engine running smoothly.

Fourth, bulletproof the forecast prior to beginning the process. Acquirers are buying your firm based on the future growth it will generate. They are a skeptical lot. When the forecast is missed, their confidence in your plan is questioned. Nothing spooks a buyer more than a quarterly miss right before the closing. The buyer wants to see strong performance right up until the closing.

Fifth, make sure that you provide enough deal support. For example, your finance team will be overwhelmed quickly. Buyers will be asking for report after report. The accuracy of the reports and the timeliness of their delivery is important. Your finance team also has a day job. During the sales process, this can be too much work for anyone. Most boutiques run lean. They are not populated with a dozen cost accountants. Consider bringing on contract assistance for the key functions to help you get through this. Many of these contractors have been through the acquisition process. They can bring some valuable tools and processes.

Lastly, it is a good idea to think about transaction preparedness. You will be asked to perform work you have never done before to support the sale. For example, you will need to prepare an information memorandum. This will include items such as incorporation documentation, employment agreements, marketing materials, and the like. Your investment bank will help you with this once the process begins. However, get your hands on a few examples. Try to put your information together and do a practice run. This will shorten the process in the early stages once you are taken to market.

Can you sustain your performance right up to closing?

1. Do you have enough backlog prior to the sales process launching?

   ☐ yes ☐ no

2. Do you have enough pipeline prior to the sales process kicking off?

   ☐ yes ☐ no

3. Can the new business team stay focused on bringing in new clients during the sales process?

   ☐ yes ☐ no

4. Can the owner's work be delegated to other team members during the sales process?

   ☐ yes ☐ no

5. Is the forecast reliable?

   ☐ yes ☐ no

6. Will the forecast remain reliable during a time of great distraction during the sales process?

   ☐ yes ☐ no

7. Have you provided enough deal support to the finance team?

   ☐ yes ☐ no

8. Can the finance team handle the constant requests for reports?

   ☐ yes ☐ no

9. Have you reviewed examples of information memorandums?

   ☐ yes ☐ no

10. Have you attempted a practice run in putting together an information memorandum?

    ☐ yes ☐ no

If you answered yes to eight or more of these questions, you could sustain performance during the sales process.

If you answered no to eight or more of these questions, you are likely to see a dip in performance during the sales process. This could result in a failed exit attempt.

## SUMMARY

The number one reason that exits fail is a decline in performance during the sales process. This should not happen to you if you prepare correctly. Selling your firm is a big project lasting almost a full year. Be sure to time it correctly and prepare yourself fully for it.

## CHAPTER 48

# MANAGING INTEREST

You are probably receiving some inbound interest in your boutique. Managing this interest correctly is very important. You get only once chance to make a first impression. There are large sums of investment capital available today. This dry powder needs to be deployed. As a result, investors have built marketing teams. These teams spend all day, every day, reaching out to owners like you. Do not overreact to calls coming in from those interested in purchasing you. These firms are kissing a lot of frogs.

How should you manage interest in your firm?

Be careful not to reveal too much information too early in the process. The idea is to create some competitive tension among possible bidders. The best way to do that is to hire an investment banker.

For those who are unfamiliar with the term *investment banker*, let me explain. An investment banker works for an investment banking firm. For example, John Doe works for Goldman Sachs, J.P. Morgan, Morgan Stanley, and others. John gets hired to advise companies looking to sell, or buy, companies. In your case, John would help you determine what your firm is worth. He and his team would prepare the marketing materials. He would reach out to a group of potential buyers. And for those interested, he would manage what is known as a process. This involves items such as arranging management meetings, reference calls, and so on. Ultimately, the investment banker is charged with getting you the best deal. They are your representation.

Boutiques attempting to sell themselves without a banker are making a mistake. The amount you save on commissions pales in comparison to the amount the banker makes you. For example, banker's fees can range from 1 percent to as high as 10 percent of the sales price. If you sell for $100 million, this is real money. However, it is not uncommon for a banker to raise the purchase price by 30 to 50 percent. What is better for you: paying 0 percent commission on a $50 million sale or paying a 3 percent commission on a $100 million sale? The first-time seller benefits from a banker in more ways than price. Boutique owners selling for the first time are inexperienced. They make costly mistakes that prevent a sale from closing. Selling for the right price is one thing. Closing the sale is another. Many deals have fallen apart late in the process due to an inexperienced seller. An investment banker will make sure that you do not shoot yourself in the foot.

Deciding on which banker to hire is a difficult decision. Here are some things to be aware of. Look for a banker with relevant transaction experience to represent your boutique. For instance, an IT services firm should choose a banker who has sold many IT services firms. Look for comparable transactions over the last four to five years. Do not settle for industry-specific experience. Be sure that the experience is niche specific. Also, size is critical. Investment bankers doing billion-dollar deals are not for you. They are unlikely to take on your project. And if they do, you will be dealing with the junior varsity team. Look for broken deals. Ask the banker how many of their assignments do not close and why. Speak directly to the owners of these companies. Hear from them why they were unsuccessful in their attempt to sell their boutiques. Seek to understand the process to develop a comprehensive buyer list. Selling boutiques is harder than selling big brand-name companies. The list of possible buyers is very long. No one banker can possibly know all the potential buyers. You need to understand how their process will surface a deep buyer pool. It is important, for instance, that the banker sources both strategic buyers and private equity buyers. Dig into the valuation range they give you. It is necessary to know how they reached these figures. Of course, it comes down to the team. Meet the actual people who will be working on your deal. As you can see, much goes into the banker selection process. However, the most important lesson is to hire one. This is not the time to do it yourself.

Another mistake made in managing interest is scaring buyers away. Boutique owners often do not have realistic price expectations. A buyer calls, the owner is flattered, and they blurt out a very high number. The buyer politely gets off the phone quickly. They feel that there is no way to get a deal done. The price is way too high and the owner is nuts. They move on to the next name on the call sheet. Your boutique is your baby. You believe that it is unique and is worth a lot. However, you do not determine the price. The market does. Your boutique is worth what someone is willing to pay for it. Nothing more and nothing less. It may make sense to suggest an initial price. This is, however, later in

**Your boutique is worth what someone is willing to pay for it. Nothing more and nothing less.**

the process. And, please, if you do, be sure it that is market based and realistic.

Buyers care a lot about deal structures. In some cases as much as price. Be careful not to scare buyers away with an unrealistic structure. It is important to understand how deals like yours are structured. For instance, selling to private equity often requires rolling over some equity. If you are unwilling to do this, many private equity firms will walk away. Or, if selling to a market leader, they will likely require an earn-out. If you are unwilling to accommodate an earn-out, your buyer pool will shrink. The market will dictate the terms. Understand the common structures and try to align with these practices. This will prevent you from running off possible buyers.

Also, understand that prices and structures change a lot. Boutique owners often overreact to opening bids. They get emotional during the process. Opening bids are not insults. They are just data inputs. The price you get should increase as you go through the process. As competitors compete for your boutique, prices go up. Unfortunately, some boutique owners get outmaneuvered by savvy buyers. At times, acquirers will throw out a big number, pending due diligence. The owner's ego becomes inflated, and they let the fox inside the hen house. The potential buyer proceeds to lower their number based on diligence findings. To the owner, it feels like a bait and switch. And, in this instance, it is. Just remember, the sales process is a nine- to twelve-month roller-coaster ride. Stay in your seat with your seat belt on.

Sometimes deals take too long and cost too much. This happens when the owner does not understand roles. For example, the banker is not the lawyer. The banker will find you a buyer and get you a deal. The attorney(s) then need to negotiate the terms. This is an additional cost and takes some time. And, like choosing a banker, selecting the right attorney matters. Do not go cheap here. You get what you pay for. The last thing you want is a lawsuit two years postsale trying claw back proceeds. Hire the best attorney you can find and let them do their job. And then there are the accountants. Deal structures can impact the tax bill a lot. You will want to keep as much of the proceeds as possible. How the transaction is booked can make a big difference. For example, did you know that a dollar amount will be assigned to your noncompete? This dollar amount will be recognized as ordinary income and not capital gains. You will pay ordinary income taxes on that in April. I did not know this at the time of my sale. But my tax lawyer and accountant did. And they negotiated down this tax liability, which saved me a lot of money. Again, you get what you pay for. Hire the best advisers you can.

As you can see, there is a lot to managing interest.

Are you prepared to do so?

1. Are investors inquiring about buying your firm?

   ☐ yes ☐ no

2. Are you making a good first impression by not divulging too much information too early?

   ☐ yes ☐ no

3. Have you created the appropriate amount of competitive tension among the buyers?

   ☐ yes ☐ no

4. Do you know who the right investment banker is for you?

   ☐ yes ☐ no

5. Have you hired them?

   ☐ yes ☐ no

6. Do you have a realistic, market-based price in your mind?

   ☐ yes ☐ no

7. Have you waited the appropriate amount of time before suggesting a price?

   ☐ yes ☐ no

8. Do you understand the typical deal structures for boutiques like yours?

   ☐ yes ☐ no

9. Are you prepared to engage and let prices drift up over time?

   ☐ yes ☐ no

10. Have you hired the best attorneys and accountants to complete the transaction?

    ☐ yes ☐ no

If you answered yes to eight or more of these questions, you are prepared to manage interest well. You are likely to make a great first impression.

If you answered no to eight or more of these questions, you are not prepared to manage interest well. You are likely to run off potential buyers during the process.

## SUMMARY

You get only one chance to make a first impression. There is a lot of available investment capital. The phone is going to ring. The email in-box is going to get pinged. The social media invitations will be coming in. Be extra careful to avoid the common mistakes made by first-time boutique sellers.

# CONCLUSION

There you have it. Approximately two hours on starting, scaling, and selling a professional services firm.

What you should do now?

I have a few suggestions.

1. *Start.* If you are thinking of starting a boutique, go. This is the golden era of professional services. The wind is at your back, and the sun is on your face. The guide in section 1 clears the hurdle of good enough. Get straight on these questions. Sign a client. Stop studying and start doing. Build a great boutique one project at a time. You can do it. Dream great dreams and make them come true.

**Build a great boutique one project at a time.**

2. *Scale.* You are past the survival stage. But you are not among the 4,100 market leaders. You can be. How far you go is determined by how badly you want it. The obstacles in your way can be overcome. The guide in section 2 should get you going. If you want more help, join Collective 54. This

is where people like you, with boutiques like yours, meet to solve problems like yours.

3. *Sell.* You built a valuable asset. It is time to hand it off to someone else. Your next life chapter is waiting for you, and it is filled with joy. It requires funding. The guide in section 3 shows you how to exit correctly. If you want your baby to land in the right hands, call Capital 54. My family office will reward you for what you built. And it will nurture your boutique with investment capital and management know-how.

APPENDIX A

# CHECKLISTS

The checklists featured in each chapter are included in this section. As in the chapters, if you answer yes to eight or more of the questions, you do not need assistance, but if you answer no to eight or more of the questions, you should make improvements.

## SECTION 1: START

### Chapter 1: The Problem

1. When you explain the problem to your family, do they understand you?

   ☐ yes ☐ no

2. When you explain the problem to friends, do they understand you?

   ☐ yes ☐ no

3. Does the problem exist in more than one industry?

   ☐ yes ☐ no

4. Does the problem exist in companies of all sizes?

   ☐ yes ☐ no

5. Does the problem exist in many geographies?

   ☐ yes ☐ no

6. Are clients paying to solve the problem today?

   ☐ yes ☐ no

7. Have clients been paying to solve this problem for years?

   ☐ yes ☐ no

8. If clients do not solve the problem, are the consequences severe?

   ☐ yes ☐ no

9. Is there a trigger event that puts clients in the market for your solution?

   ☐ yes ☐ no

10. When clients have the problem, do they work to get it solved by a deadline?

    ☐ yes ☐ no

## Chapter 2: The Client

1. Do you have a demographic profile for your target client?

   ☐ yes ☐ no

2. Do you have a psychographic profile for your client?

   ☐ yes ☐ no

3. Do you have an elevator pitch that speaks directly to the client?

   ☐ yes ☐ no

4. Do you understand the personal goals of the client?

   ☐ yes ☐ no

5. Do you understand the professional goals of the client?

   ☐ yes ☐ no

6. Do you understand the obstacles preventing the client from accomplishing the personal goals?

   ☐ yes ☐ no

7. Do you understand the obstacles preventing the client from accomplishing the professional goals?

   ☐ yes ☐ no

8. Do you understand the likely objections that your client is going to submit to you?

   ☐ yes ☐ no

9. Do you understand the client's top priorities?

   ☐ yes ☐ no

10. Do you understand the emotional makeup of the client?

   ☐ yes ☐ no

## Chapter 3: The Competitors

1. Can you calculate a client's cost of inaction?

   ☐ yes ☐ no

2. Can you find a compelling event that puts a deadline on the client's project?

   ☐ yes ☐ no

3. Are you confident enough to guarantee your work?

   ☐ yes ☐ no

4. Can you establish your credibility in the eyes of your client?

   ☐ yes ☐ no

5. Can you signal quality to the client by delivering a best-in-class proposal?

   ☐ yes ☐ no

6. Can you deliver much faster than the market leaders in your niche?

   ☐ yes ☐ no

7. Can you earn healthy margins and still be 25 percent less than the market leaders?

   ☐ yes ☐ no

8. Are you more enjoyable to work with than the market leaders?

   ☐ yes ☐ no

9. Do you understand the alternative solutions to the problem you address?

   ☐ yes ☐ no

10. Will a postmortem reveal to the client that these alternatives have a poor track record?

   ☐ yes ☐ no

## Chapter 4: The Revenue

1. Will a client pay you more than $500 per hour?

   ☐ yes ☐ no

2. Will a client pay you in advance to secure your service on demand?

   ☐ yes ☐ no

3. Can you scope your projects with precision?

   ☐ yes ☐ no

4. Can you prove direct attribution of results in your engagements?

   ☐ yes ☐ no

5. Will your clients pay you for the privilege of speaking to your other clients?

   ☐ yes ☐ no

6. Will your clients pay you for the right to use your intellectual property?

   ☐ yes ☐ no

7. Do you have proprietary data that clients would like to subscribe to?

   ☐ yes ☐ no

8. Do you put on events, and are clients willing to buy tickets to attend?

   ☐ yes ☐ no

9. Are other boutiques willing to pay you a royalty to distribute your intellectual property?

   ☐ yes ☐ no

10. Does your business model include at least three sources of revenue?

    ☐ yes ☐ no

## Chapter 5: The Service

1. Are you offering a service that clients are already buying?

   ☐ yes ☐ no

2. Are there many legacy firms providing this service?

   ☐ yes ☐ no

3. Are these legacy firms ripe for disruption?

   ☐ yes ☐ no

4. Can you use less expensive labor to deliver it?

   ☐ yes ☐ no

5. Can you use technology automation to streamline it?

   ☐ yes ☐ no

6. Can you perform the service better than the alternatives?

   ☐ yes ☐ no

7. Can you perform the service faster than the alternatives?

   ☐ yes ☐ no

8. Can you perform the service cheaper than the alternatives?

   ☐ yes ☐ no

9. Can you combine better/faster/cheaper into a single value proposition?

   ☐ yes ☐ no

10. Are you staying away from the latest fad that might not have staying power?

    ☐ yes ☐ no

## Chapter 6: The Go-to-Market

1. Is it obvious to prospects who you serve and how you serve them?

   ☐ yes ☐ no

2. Is it obvious to prospects why you are the best at what you do?

   ☐ yes ☐ no

3. Are you in front of enough prospects to hit your revenue targets?

   ☐ yes ☐ no

4. Do you understand how clients decide to hire someone like you?

   ☐ yes ☐ no

5. Can you consistently win more than 50 percent of the time?

   ☐ yes ☐ no

6. Are you extending your reach through multiple marketing channels?

   ☐ yes ☐ no

7. Are you and your team motivated to bring in revenue?

   ☐ yes ☐ no

8. Are you and your team highly trained to win new business?

   ☐ yes ☐ no

9. Are you covering your market sufficiently?

   ☐ yes ☐ no

10. Do you have an agency capable of multiplying your efforts?

   ☐ yes ☐ no

## Chapter 7: The Engagement

1. Do you want to serve a small number of clients?

   ☐ yes ☐ no

2. Do you want to live and die on the big deal?

   ☐ yes ☐ no

3. Can you handle the lumpiness that comes with elephant

hunting?

☐ yes ☐ no

4. Do you want to stay engaged with clients for an extended time period?

   ☐ yes ☐ no

5. Can you get in front of big companies that can afford very large projects?

   ☐ yes ☐ no

6. Can you hire the expensive talent needed to deliver expensive projects?

   ☐ yes ☐ no

7. Can your cash flow support periods of time with low utilization rates?

   ☐ yes ☐ no

8. Is the problem you solve complex enough to warrant long engagements?

   ☐ yes ☐ no

9. Is the service you offer robust enough to require expensive engagements?

   ☐ yes ☐ no

10. Are you comfortable with the risk that comes from high revenue concentration?

    ☐ yes ☐ no

## Chapter 8: The Market

1. Are there thousands of targets to pursue?

   ☐ yes ☐ no

2. Are they reachable?

   ☐ yes ☐ no

3. When they are reached, will they consider you?

   ☐ yes ☐ no

4. Can you win your fair share of the opportunities?

   ☐ yes ☐ no

5. Can you win your fair share consistently?

   ☐ yes ☐ no

6. When you do win, is the amount of money spent worth the pursuit?

   ☐ yes ☐ no

7. Is the market large enough to support your boutique, assuming modest penetration rates?

   ☐ yes ☐ no

8. Are there new targets to pursue each year—that is, is the market growing?

   ☐ yes ☐ no

9. Can you drive up the engagement size over time?

   ☐ yes ☐ no

10. Will there be a reasonable rate of repeat purchases?

   ☐ yes ☐ no

## Chapter 9: The Team

1. Does your founding team consist of three or more partners?

   ☐ yes ☐ no

2. Is there no overlap in skills among the founding partners?

   ☐ yes ☐ no

3. Is there a loss in capacity due to confusion over who is doing what?

   ☐ yes ☐ no

4. Do you have a partner responsible for acquiring clients?

   ☐ yes ☐ no

5. Do you have a partner responsible for servicing clients?

   ☐ yes ☐ no

6. Do you have a partner responsible for developing service lines?

   ☐ yes ☐ no

7. Can the partner who owns the service department scale to dozens of employees?

   ☐ yes ☐ no

8. Can the partner who owns the marketing and sales department handle big egos?

   ☐ yes ☐ no

9. Is the partner who owns service development comfortable being a lone wolf?

   ☐ yes ☐ no

10. Do the partners complement, rather than compete, with one another?

    ☐ yes ☐ no

## SECTION 2: SCALE

### Chapter 10: Scale Capital

1. Are you generating enough free cash flow to fund scale?

   ☐ yes ☐ no

2. Do you know where to deploy this extra free cash flow?

   ☐ yes ☐ no

3. Are you willing to go without today for scale tomorrow?

   ☐ yes ☐ no

4. Have you been in business for at least five years?

   ☐ yes ☐ no

5. Are you generating stable EBITDA every year?

   ☐ yes ☐ no

6. Would two to three times EBITDA be enough to fund your scale?

   ☐ yes ☐ no

7. Can your P&L handle the debt service burden of a loan?

   ☐ yes ☐ no

8. Are you willing to personally guarantee a loan?

   ☐ yes ☐ no

9. Do you have enough personal assets to secure the loan if open to a guarantee?

   ☐ yes ☐ no

10. Are you willing to dilute your ownership stake for the right equity partner?

    ☐ yes ☐ no

## Chapter 11: Leverage

1. Is your leverage of employee to owner at least 10:1?

   ☐ yes ☐ no

2. Is the proper mix of low, middle, and senior staff clear to you?

   ☐ yes ☐ no

3. Do you understand the skills mix required for an engagement before you sign it?

   ☐ yes ☐ no

4. Do you understand which revenue is "good" and which is "bad"?

   ☐ yes ☐ no

5. Do you have a zero-tolerance policy for one-off projects?

   ☐ yes ☐ no

6. Do the partners/owners work on the business instead of in the business?

   ☐ yes ☐ no

7. Do your service offerings come with procedure manuals for the delivery staff?

   ☐ yes ☐ no

8. Do you assign work to project teams strategically versus reactionary?

   ☐ yes ☐ no

9. Does your hiring plan forecast demand for a specific leverage ratio?

   ☐ yes ☐ no

10. Do your financial goals match up with the leverage ratio assumptions in your business plan?

    ☐ yes ☐ no

## Chapter 12: Cash Flow

1. Will you run out of working capital if you double your firm?

   ☐ yes ☐ no

2. Will you need a lot of short-term debt if you double your firm?

   ☐ yes ☐ no

3. Will you develop a collections problem if you double your firm?

   ☐ yes ☐ no

4. Will your cash payments exceed your cash income if you double your firm?

   ☐ yes ☐ no

5. Will you have a hard time getting enough cash on the balance sheet to double your firm?

   ☐ yes ☐ no

6. When growth has spiked in the past, did your cash flow ever turn negative?

   ☐ yes ☐ no

7. Will payroll growth exceed accounts receivable growth when you double your boutique?

   ☐ yes ☐ no

8. Will cash flow problems be hidden due to lack of forward visibility?

   ☐ yes ☐ no

9. Will it be hard to generate yield on your cash deposits?

   ☐ yes ☐ no

10. Will you be at risk of paying your future obligations if you double your firm?

   ☐ yes ☐ no

## Chapter 13: Life Cycle

1. Do your clients hire you for never-before-seen problems?

   ☐ yes ☐ no

2. Do you employ leading experts in the field?

   ☐ yes ☐ no

3. Do you have legally protected intellectual property?

   ☐ yes ☐ no

4. Do your clients hire you because you have solved their problem before?

   ☐ yes ☐ no

5. Do your clients hire you because you have direct, relevant case studies?

   ☐ yes ☐ no

6. Do your clients hire you because you help them avoid common mistakes?

   ☐ yes ☐ no

7. Do your clients hire you because they are busy and need an extra pair of hands?

   ☐ yes ☐ no

8. Do your clients hire you because you can get the work done quickly?

   ☐ yes ☐ no

9. Do your clients hire you because you have an army of trained people to deploy immediately?

   ☐ yes ☐ no

10. Do your service offerings start out as leading edge and over time become commodities?

    ☐ yes ☐ no

## Chapter 14: Yield

1. Are your average utilization rates above 85 percent?

   ☐ yes ☐ no

2. Senior staff above 70 percent?

   ☐ yes ☐ no

3. Midlevel staff above 80 percent?

   ☐ yes ☐ no

4. Junior staff above 90 percent?

   ☐ yes ☐ no

5. Are your average fees above $400?

   ☐ yes ☐ no

6. Senior staff above $750?

   ☐ yes ☐ no

7. Midlevel staff above $500?

   ☐ yes ☐ no

8. Junior staff above $250?

   ☐ yes ☐ no

9. Are you assuming at least forty-eight weeks and forty hours per week?

   ☐ yes ☐ no

10. Are you distinguished from the generalist with three to five forms of specialization?

    ☐ yes ☐ no

## Chapter 15: Pricing

1. Do you know what your offering is worth to clients?

   ☐ yes ☐ no

2. Can you quantify the value of your work in hard dollars?

   ☐ yes ☐ no

3. Do you know what clients are willing to pay for your services?

   ☐ yes ☐ no

4. Can you explain the logic of your pricing in a way that makes sense to clients?

   ☐ yes ☐ no

5. Does your price illustrate to the client the link between price and value?

   ☐ yes ☐ no

6. Do you charge the most for the service features that your clients want the most?

   ☐ yes ☐ no

7. Do you charge the least for the service features that your clients don't care much about?

   ☐ yes ☐ no

8. Do you allow your clients to choose their price by presenting options?

   ☐ yes ☐ no

9. Is your sales team skilled at overcoming price objections?

   ☐ yes ☐ no

10. Have you built into your system an annual price increase?

    ☐ yes ☐ no

## Chapter 16: Replication

1. Do you feel like you must do everything yourself?

   ☐ yes ☐ no

2. Do you feel like you must be in every key meeting?

   ☐ yes ☐ no

3. Do clients require you to be directly involved in their projects?

   ☐ yes ☐ no

4. Do your employees come to you for help constantly?

   ☐ yes ☐ no

5. Do you have to micromanage everyone?

   ☐ yes ☐ no

6. Do you have to review everything before it goes out?

   ☐ yes ☐ no

7. Are you working too much?

   ☐ yes ☐ no

8. Is it faster to just do the work yourself?

   ☐ yes ☐ no

9. Do you feel like it will get done correctly only if you do it?

   ☐ yes ☐ no

10. Are you turning over employees?

   ☐ yes ☐ no

## Chapter 17: Culture

1. Is your culture important to the success of your boutique?

   ☐ yes ☐ no

2. Does every employee understand the "way things get done around here"?

   ☐ yes ☐ no

3. Does every employee understand what you are trying to

accomplish?

☐ yes ☐ no

4. Does every employee understand how they personally contribute to these goals?

   ☐ yes ☐ no

5. Is it clear which behaviors are rewarded?

   ☐ yes ☐ no

6. Is it clear which behaviors are punished?

   ☐ yes ☐ no

7. Is it clear which function inside the boutique is the dominant function?

   ☐ yes ☐ no

8. Is the leader of this function the leader of the boutique?

   ☐ yes ☐ no

9. Is the culture scaling naturally the way you want it to?

   ☐ yes ☐ no

10. Are you nurturing the culture as you scale?

    ☐ yes ☐ no

## Chapter 18: Business Development

1. Are you generating a lot of business from existing clients?

   ☐ yes ☐ no

2. Have you reduced your need for new clients substantially?

   ☐ yes ☐ no

3. Do you understand your share of wallet for your current clients?

   ☐ yes ☐ no

4. Are your current clients up to date on your full capabilities?

   ☐ yes ☐ no

5. Are you investing nonbillable hours directly into your existing clients?

   ☐ yes ☐ no

6. Have you redesigned your business development process to prioritize existing clients?

   ☐ yes ☐ no

7. Have you trained your employees on the new business development process?

   ☐ yes ☐ no

8. Are your "delivery teams" goaled and measured on finding new opportunities?

   ☐ yes ☐ no

9. Are the employees who are best at business development your cultural heroes?

   ☐ yes ☐ no

10. Do you make sure that your current clients know how important they are to you?

    ☐ yes ☐ no

## Chapter 19: Service Offering Development

1. Is your growth dependent on increasing revenue from existing clients?

   ☐ yes ☐ no

2. Do you need new reasons to remain relevant to your clients?

☐ yes ☐ no

3. Do your clients eventually get fatigued?

   ☐ yes ☐ no

4. Do you know what your clients need?

   ☐ yes ☐ no

5. Can you continuously learn what your clients need?

   ☐ yes ☐ no

6. Would your clients participate on a client advisory board?

   ☐ yes ☐ no

7. Can you implement postproject reviews?

   ☐ yes ☐ no

8. Can you perform client satisfaction reviews after every project?

   ☐ yes ☐ no

9. Can you perform win-loss reviews after every sales campaign?

   ☐ yes ☐ no

10. Are there relevant industry conferences that you can attend?

   ☐ yes ☐ no

## Chapter 20: The Client Experience

1. Have you documented the client experience journey?

   ☐ yes ☐ no

2. Do each of your clients feel that they are important to you?

   ☐ yes ☐ no

3. Do you understand the emotional context of the client during an engagement?

   ☐ yes ☐ no

4. Do clients know why you are doing what you are doing?

   ☐ yes ☐ no

5. Do clients feel that they are part of the engagement team?

   ☐ yes ☐ no

6. Do clients know what is going to happen next before it happens?

   ☐ yes ☐ no

7. Do you research meeting attendees prior to each meeting?

   ☐ yes ☐ no

8. Do you send prereading material to clients in enough time?

   ☐ yes ☐ no

9. Do you make it easy for clients to use your materials internally?

   ☐ yes ☐ no

10. Do you call the client after every meeting to confirm that goals were met?

   ☐ yes ☐ no

## Chapter 21: Organizational Structure

1. Can you decouple the rate of revenue growth from the rate of employee growth?

   ☐ yes ☐ no

2. Are most of your problems people related?

   ☐ yes ☐ no

3. Is payroll your biggest expense?

   ☐ yes ☐ no

4. Can technology perform work that humans are doing today?

   ☐ yes ☐ no

5. Are you offshoring less than 40 percent of your work?

   ☐ yes ☐ no

6. Can you flex up/flex down head count to match demand close to real time?

   ☐ yes ☐ no

7. Are you skilled at labor arbitrage?

   ☐ yes ☐ no

8. Is it clear that scale does not refer to the number of employees but to the amount of cash flow?

   ☐ yes ☐ no

9. Is it hard to match revenue and expenses?

   ☐ yes ☐ no

10. Do you have limited forward visibility in your business?

    ☐ yes ☐ no

## Chapter 22: Recruiting

1. Do individual contributors need to evolve into managers?

   ☐ yes ☐ no

2. Do managers need to evolve into managers of managers?

   ☐ yes ☐ no

3. Do managers of managers need to evolve into executives?

   ☐ yes ☐ no

4. Do you need to shift from generalists to specialists?

   ☐ yes ☐ no

5. Are you attracting sophisticated clients with higher expectations?

   ☐ yes ☐ no

6. Has the founder become a bottleneck?

   ☐ yes ☐ no

7. Can the impact of the founder be amplified if partnered with a CEO?

   ☐ yes ☐ no

8. Does decision-making need to get pushed to those closest to the clients?

   ☐ yes ☐ no

9. Is it time to shift from experimenting with the model to scaling the model?

   ☐ yes ☐ no

10. Is it true that "what got you here won't get you there"?

    ☐ yes ☐ no

## Chapter 23: Partner Pay

1. Are you paying salaries based on external benchmarks?

   ☐ yes ☐ no

2. Are you paying salaries at the midpoint of the benchmarks?

   ☐ yes ☐ no

3. Are years of service a fair way to pay partners?

   ☐ yes ☐ no

4. Are senior partners' past contributions contributing to today's wealth creation?

   ☐ yes ☐ no

5. Will the younger partners stick around to wait for the senior partners to retire?

   ☐ yes ☐ no

6. Do you have clear objectives for each partner?

   ☐ yes ☐ no

7. Is it clear when the objectives are met?

   ☐ yes ☐ no

8. Is it possible to balance short-term and long-term wealth creation with these objectives?

   ☐ yes ☐ no

9. Will partners perform with integrity if placed on the bonus jury?

   ☐ yes ☐ no

10. Can you develop a methodology that fairly attributes wealth creation to partner activities?

    ☐ yes ☐ no

## Chapter 24: Equity

1. Is your firm owned by more than one person?

   ☐ yes ☐ no

2. Do the owners contribute to wealth creation in different proportions?

   ☐ yes ☐ no

3. Are the owners at different stages in life?

   ☐ yes ☐ no

4. Do the owners have different financial needs?

   ☐ yes ☐ no

5. Do the owners have different visions of the future?

   ☐ yes ☐ no

6. Have the partner contributions fluctuated over the years?

   ☐ yes ☐ no

7. Has resentment crept into the relationships?

   ☐ yes ☐ no

8. Are you living with a legacy ownership structure that is now outdated?

   ☐ yes ☐ no

9. Will rising stars require ownership to be retained?

   ☐ yes ☐ no

10. Has the ownership structure distorted policy making?

   ☐ yes ☐ no

## Chapter 25: Power

1. Have you transitioned from start-up to boutique?

   ☐ yes ☐ no

2. Are you attempting to become a market leader—that is, one of the 4,100?

   ☐ yes ☐ no

3. Do you have a dictator in place?

   ☐ yes ☐ no

4. Have the dictator's once great instincts begun to deteriorate?

   ☐ yes ☐ no

5. Have the number of decisions to be made gone up considerably?

   ☐ yes ☐ no

6. Has the complexity of the decisions to be made increased substantially?

   ☐ yes ☐ no

7. Does it make sense to distribute authority close to the client?

   ☐ yes ☐ no

8. Do the employees want a greater say in policy making?

   ☐ yes ☐ no

9. Do the owners want to delegate decision-making more?

   ☐ yes ☐ no

10. Do you have a person capable of serving as a managing partner?

    ☐ yes ☐ no

## Chapter 26: Strategy

1. Does it outline how the firm will develop new capabilities that the competitors do not have?

   ☐ yes ☐ no

2. Does it detail why the competitors cannot match them?

   ☐ yes ☐ no

3. Does it specify how these capabilities will be pushed into the market?

   ☐ yes ☐ no

4. Does it explain how your capital is being allocated (people,

money, and time)?

☐ yes ☐ no

5. Does it specify how this capital allocation plan is different from the competitors?

   ☐ yes ☐ no

6. Is the strategy supported by enough client-sourced evidence?

   ☐ yes ☐ no

7. Does the strategy specify who oversees each program?

   ☐ yes ☐ no

8. Has the team been properly incented to execute the plan?

   ☐ yes ☐ no

9. Does it detail how the competitors plan to beat you?

   ☐ yes ☐ no

10. Does it specify how you plan to respond to competitor attacks?

    ☐ yes ☐ no

# SECTION 3: SELL

## Chapter 27: Why Sell?

1. Do you have a clear vision of your future?

   ☐ yes ☐ no

2. Does selling your boutique help you get there?

   ☐ yes ☐ no

3. Do you know why you do what you do?

   ☐ yes ☐ no

4. Would selling the firm bring you closer to your purpose?

   ☐ yes ☐ no

5. Do you have a set of values that define how you want to behave?

   ☐ yes ☐ no

6. Would the sale of your boutique allow you to behave the way you want?

   ☐ yes ☐ no

7. Do you know the type of community you want to be a part of?

   ☐ yes ☐ no

8. Would selling your firm allow you to spend time with these people?

   ☐ yes ☐ no

9. Will the proceeds of the sale fund something more than material possessions?

   ☐ yes ☐ no

10. Are you personally prepared for the next chapter of your life?

   ☐ yes ☐ no

## Chapter 28: Mistakes

1. Do you know what you want from the sale?

   ☐ yes ☐ no

2. Do you know what you are going to do after the sale?

   ☐ yes ☐ no

3. Is your business attractive to a buyer?

   ☐ yes ☐ no

4. Do you have a sellable boutique?

   ☐ yes ☐ no

5. Do you have a handpicked successor?

   ☐ yes ☐ no

6. Is the successor ready to take over?

   ☐ yes ☐ no

7. Have you lined up an all-star team of advisers to help you?

   ☐ yes ☐ no

8. Are you prepared for the postsale criticism headed your way?

   ☐ yes ☐ no

9. Do you understand who you are selling your boutique to?

   ☐ yes ☐ no

10. Do you understand their motives for buying?

    ☐ yes ☐ no

## Chapter 29: Market Position

1. Is your average fee level about $500 per hour?

   ☐ yes ☐ no

2. If not, can you prove that you are not a body shop?

   ☐ yes ☐ no

3. Is your fee volume big enough to prove that you are in a large market?

   ☐ yes ☐ no

4. If not, can you prove that you are in a large and growing market, with a lot of runway?

   ☐ yes ☐ no

5. Do you have a clear client return on investment?

   ☐ yes ☐ no

6. If not, can you prove that your clients realize a good cost-benefit trade-off?

   ☐ yes ☐ no

7. Do you call on the board of directors of your target client?

   ☐ yes ☐ no

8. Do you call on the CEO of your target client?

   ☐ yes ☐ no

9. Did your financial performance hold up well during the last recession?

   ☐ yes ☐ no

10. Can you prove to a potential acquirer that your boutique is cycle resilient?

    ☐ yes ☐ no

## Chapter 30: Growth

1. Are you growing revenue faster than your boutique competitors?

   ☐ yes ☐ no

2. Have you been doing so for a few years?

   ☐ yes ☐ no

3. Are you growing your profits faster than your boutique competitors?

   ☐ yes ☐ no

4. Have you been doing so for a few years?

   ☐ yes ☐ no

5. Are you growing your revenue faster than the practice inside the large market leaders?

   ☐ yes ☐ no

6. Have you been doing so for a few years?

   ☐ yes ☐ no

7. Are you growing your profits faster than the practice inside the large market leaders?

   ☐ yes ☐ no

8. Have you been doing so for a few years?

   ☐ yes ☐ no

9. Are you growing your cash balance to cover payroll for twelve months?

   ☐ yes ☐ no

10. Do you have at least twelve months of forward visibility?

   ☐ yes ☐ no

## Chapter 31: Client Relationships

1. Are your client relationships an asset on your balance sheet?

   ☐ yes ☐ no

2. Is this asset appreciating in value?

   ☐ yes ☐ no

3. Do you have a diversified client base, with no one client worth more than 10 percent of revenue?

   ☐ yes ☐ no

4. Does the tenure of your client relationships exceed three years?

   ☐ yes ☐ no

5. Are your clients' businesses stable?

   ☐ yes ☐ no

6. Are your clients' end relationships stable?

   ☐ yes ☐ no

7. Do you have account plans?

   ☐ yes ☐ no

8. Have you institutionalized your client relationships into a customer relationship management system?

   ☐ yes ☐ no

9. Are the client relationships with the firm and not with the key employee?

   ☐ yes ☐ no

10. Will the billings from your client relationships stay when the key employee quits?

   ☐ yes ☐ no

## Chapter 32: Fee Quality

1. Do you generate about 60 percent of your fees from existing clients?

   ☐ yes ☐ no

2. Do you generate approximately 40 percent of your fees from new clients?

   ☐ yes ☐ no

3. Is the average client contract longer than twelve months?

   ☐ yes ☐ no

4. Do your projects naturally build on one another?

   ☐ yes ☐ no

5. Is your service built to pull through upsell?

   ☐ yes ☐ no

6. Is your service designed to pull through cross sell?

   ☐ yes ☐ no

7. Are your fees predictable?

   ☐ yes ☐ no

8. Do you collect your fee in advance of performing the work?

   ☐ yes ☐ no

9. Can you fund your growth from free cash flow?

   ☐ yes ☐ no

10. Can you pay the bills without using debt?

    ☐ yes ☐ no

## Chapter 33: Intellectual Property

1. Do you have any patents?

   ☐ yes ☐ no

2. Do you have any copyrights?

   ☐ yes ☐ no

3. Do you have any trademarks?

   ☐ yes ☐ no

4. Are you generating revenue by granting the right to use your intellectual property to anyone?

   ☐ yes ☐ no

5. Are you collecting data that clients will pay to have access to?

   ☐ yes ☐ no

6. Are you inventing methodologies that third parties will pay to be able to use?

   ☐ yes ☐ no

7. Are you coding your knowledge into licensable application tools?

   ☐ yes ☐ no

8. Will individuals pay you for a certification to validate their skills?

   ☐ yes ☐ no

9. Are you a true professional service firm and not a body shop?

   ☐ yes ☐ no

10. Is it clear to a potential buyer that your boutique is not just a well-run lifestyle business?

    ☐ yes ☐ no

## Chapter 34: Sales and Marketing Process

1. Are the owners removed from the sales process?

   ☐ yes ☐ no

2. Are employees generating all the sales?

   ☐ yes ☐ no

3. Is business being generated from scalable sources in addition to referrals?

   ☐ yes ☐ no

4. Have sales increased consistently without adding partners/owners?

   ☐ yes ☐ no

5. Have your financials been able to handle the expense of a commercial sales team?

   ☐ yes ☐ no

6. Have the sales results from the commercial sales team been consistent over time?

   ☐ yes ☐ no

7. Have the win rates with the commercial sales team been on par with the partners'?

   ☐ yes ☐ no

8. Have the deal sizes with the commercial sales team been on par with the partners'?

   ☐ yes ☐ no

9. Have the sales cycle lengths with the commercial sales team been on par with the partners'?

   ☐ yes ☐ no

10. Can the commercial sales team be expanded significantly without breaking the boutique?

   ☐ yes ☐ no

## Chapter 35: Employee Loyalty

1. Is your turnover rate 15 percent or lower?

   ☐ yes ☐ no

2. Is the average tenure of your employees greater than five years?

   ☐ yes ☐ no

3. Do most of your promotions get filled internally?

   ☐ yes ☐ no

4. Do you have an in-house recruiting engine that provides you with a stream of quality people?

   ☐ yes ☐ no

5. Do you get rewarded by your employees with their discretionary effort?

   ☐ yes ☐ no

6. Does your boutique have a purpose that the employees believe in?

   ☐ yes ☐ no

7. Does your boutique have a vision of the future that employees want to be a part of?

   ☐ yes ☐ no

8. Does your boutique have a set of values, and are they lived by?

   ☐ yes ☐ no

9. Are you paying your employees what they are worth?

   ☐ yes ☐ no

10. Will your former employees sing your praises when contacted?

    ☐ yes ☐ no

## Chapter 36: Management Quality

1. Is the management team staying with the business postsale?

   ☐ yes ☐ no

2. Is there an industrial-strength strategy developed that an investor can bet on?

   ☐ yes ☐ no

3. Does management quality go at least one layer deep in the organizational chart?

   ☐ yes ☐ no

4. Does the management team drive the strategy deep into the boutique?

   ☐ yes ☐ no

5. Are there cascading targets that reach all the way to the frontline employees?

   ☐ yes ☐ no

6. Is there a believable vision of the future?

   ☐ yes ☐ no

7. Is the management team capable of getting the boutique to this future state?

   ☐ yes ☐ no

8. Is the management team excited and passionate about attempting to do so?

   ☐ yes ☐ no

9. Have all the holes in the team been addressed?

   ☐ yes ☐ no

10. Do the forward projections reflect the true cost to operate the firm in the future?

   ☐ yes ☐ no

## Chapter 37: Culture Fit

1. Is the founder still involved in the business?

   ☐ yes ☐ no

2. Does the founder's origin story shed a light on the bou-

tique's culture?

☐ yes ☐ no

3. Are the boutique's legends still involved in the business?

   ☐ yes ☐ no

4. Do they personify the boutique's culture?

   ☐ yes ☐ no

5. Does the boutique work well across functions?

   ☐ yes ☐ no

6. Do the artifacts indicate the boutique's culture?

   ☐ yes ☐ no

7. Do employees who are cultural mismatches get rejected by the boutique?

   ☐ yes ☐ no

8. Do the boutique's best clients share a set of common beliefs with the boutique?

   ☐ yes ☐ no

9. Are there deep relationships between the legends and the best clients?

   ☐ yes ☐ no

10. Is it clear to a potential acquirer how your boutique behaves?

    ☐ yes ☐ no

## Chapter 38: Organizational Design

1. Will your organizational model be easy to absorb?

   ☐ yes ☐ no

2. Are you organized around either geography, industry, or

function?

☐ yes ☐ no

3. Have you steered clear of the matrix?

   ☐ yes ☐ no

4. Are you large enough to be interesting but small enough to integrate easily?

   ☐ yes ☐ no

5. Does your organizational model reflect the niche you serve?

   ☐ yes ☐ no

6. Does your organizational model reflect your business model?

   ☐ yes ☐ no

7. Is the organizational model a good starting point for an easy integration?

   ☐ yes ☐ no

8. Is your organizational model flexible enough to morph into somebody else's?

   ☐ yes ☐ no

9. Does the organizational model reflect the true cost to operate your boutique?

   ☐ yes ☐ no

10. Will it be obvious to a potential acquirer where the synergies will come from?

    ☐ yes ☐ no

## Chapter 39: Continuous Improvement

1. Do you version control your methodologies?

   ☐ yes ☐ no

2. Do you progressively certify your employees?

   ☐ yes ☐ no

3. Are you charging existing clients more for the same service?

   ☐ yes ☐ no

4. Are your client satisfaction scores trending up over time?

   ☐ yes ☐ no

5. Are your employee engagement scores trending up over time?

   ☐ yes ☐ no

6. Are your profit margins trending up over time?

   ☐ yes ☐ no

7. Have your engagement models moved from on-site to virtual, at least partially?

   ☐ yes ☐ no

8. Have client deliverables been digitized?

   ☐ yes ☐ no

9. Have your price levels trended up over time?

   ☐ yes ☐ no

10. Has the quality of your client roster improved over time?

    ☐ yes ☐ no

## Chapter 40: Innovation

1. Have you pioneered a new approach in your niche?

   ☐ yes ☐ no

2. Are you more than a one-hit wonder?

   ☐ yes ☐ no

3. Has your industry adopted your way of doing things?

   ☐ yes ☐ no

4. Does your industry use your language as its own?

   ☐ yes ☐ no

5. Do the smartest in your niche come to you with the most challenging issues?

   ☐ yes ☐ no

6. Has an ecosystem of boutiques formed around your innovation?

   ☐ yes ☐ no

7. Do you mainstage the keynote for the most important industry conference?

   ☐ yes ☐ no

8. Do you get more than $50,000 for a speech?

   ☐ yes ☐ no

9. Do employees join your firm for the opportunity to work next to you?

   ☐ yes ☐ no

10. Have you created a legacy that will live on in your niche after you leave?

    ☐ yes ☐ no

## Chapter 41: Financial Market Trends

1. Are there large pools of available capital in your niche?

   ☐ yes ☐ no

2. Are the multiyear industry trends of your niche favorable?

   ☐ yes ☐ no

3. Are banks lending in your niche?

   ☐ yes ☐ no

4. Are private lending institutions interested in your niche?

   ☐ yes ☐ no

5. Are the interest rates attractive?

   ☐ yes ☐ no

6. Can your boutique handle a decent amount of debt on the balance sheet?

   ☐ yes ☐ no

7. Are deals happening in your space?

   ☐ yes ☐ no

8. Do you know the drivers of this deal activity?

   ☐ yes ☐ no

9. Are you at the right point in the economic cycle?

   ☐ yes ☐ no

10. If they had to, would a buyer make you an all-cash offer?

    ☐ yes ☐ no

## Chapter 42: Comparables

1. Do you have a list of boutiques in your category that recently sold?

   ☐ yes ☐ no

2. Do you know the price paid for each?

   ☐ yes ☐ no

3. Do you know the deal terms for each?

   ☐ yes ☐ no

4. Do you know the investment banker who represented each?

   ☐ yes ☐ no

5. Do you know the names of the investors who bid on each?

   ☐ yes ☐ no

6. Do you know who won the big for each?

   ☐ yes ☐ no

7. Do you know exactly why the winner won?

   ☐ yes ☐ no

8. Is your boutique in the correct category?

   ☐ yes ☐ no

9. Is the correct category for your boutique obvious to potential buyers?

   ☐ yes ☐ no

10. Are you trying to sell your boutique to the right group of buyers?

    ☐ yes ☐ no

## Chapter 43: Universe of Buyers

1. Do you know how many firms like yours are for sale?

   ☐ yes ☐ no

2. Have you completed a market map?

   ☐ yes ☐ no

3. Has this map produced an exhaustive list of potential buyers?

   ☐ yes ☐ no

4. Has this map produced an exhaustive list of potential buyers from adjacent markets?

   ☐ yes ☐ no

5. Has this list been augmented with private equity firms with a known interest in boutiques like yours?

   ☐ yes ☐ no

6. Have you developed a compelling strategic rationale to buy your boutique?

   ☐ yes ☐ no

7. Has this strategic rationale been customized for each potential buyer?

   ☐ yes ☐ no

8. Do you know who the leading investment bank is in your niche?

   ☐ yes ☐ no

9. Have you approached them about representing your boutique?

   ☐ yes ☐ no

10. Has the investment bank creatively enlarged the universe of potential buyers?

    ☐ yes ☐ no

## Chapter 44: De-Risk

1. Do you have five years of audited financials?

   ☐ yes ☐ no

2. Do you have five years of tax returns?

   ☐ yes ☐ no

3. Are you operating according to industry-standard accounting principles?

   ☐ yes ☐ no

4. Do you have few, if any, add backs?

   ☐ yes ☐ no

5. Is your personal financial life clearly separated from the business financials?

   ☐ yes ☐ no

6. Have you never been sued?

   ☐ yes ☐ no

7. Have you never sued anyone?

   ☐ yes ☐ no

8. Are you clear of any outstanding legal action?

   ☐ yes ☐ no

9. Are you using industry-standard legal contracts with clients, employees, and suppliers?

   ☐ yes ☐ no

10. Are you compliant with industry regulations?

   ☐ yes ☐ no

## Chapter 45: Buy versus Build

1. Has the market shifted, creating a gap in the service portfolios of your market leaders?

   ☐ yes ☐ no

2. Are the market leaders you compete with aware of the gap?

   ☐ yes ☐ no

3. Is the gap urgent?

   ☐ yes ☐ no

4. Have you directly competed with a market leader on a deal in this specific gap area?

   ☐ yes ☐ no

5. Did you win?

   ☐ yes ☐ no

6. Does the market leader know they lost to you?

   ☐ yes ☐ no

7. Do they know they lost because you have a capabilities advantage over them?

   ☐ yes ☐ no

8. If they were to fill the gap, would it be fastest to buy you?

   ☐ yes ☐ no

9. If they were to fill the gap, would it be cheaper to buy you than to build internally?

   ☐ yes ☐ no

10. Are the chances of successfully filling the gap better if they buy you?

    ☐ yes ☐ no

## Chapter 46: Shareholder and Stakeholder Alignment

1. Do you have more than one shareholder?

   ☐ yes ☐ no

2. Do they agree on an acceptable price?

   ☐ yes ☐ no

3. Do they agree on the terms of a deal?

   ☐ yes ☐ no

4. Are their expectations realistic?

   ☐ yes ☐ no

5. Do you have multiple stakeholder groups?

   ☐ yes ☐ no

6. Do you know what each stakeholder group wants?

   ☐ yes ☐ no

7. Are their expectations realistic?

   ☐ yes ☐ no

8. Do you know which stakeholder groups can get in the way of your sale?

   ☐ yes ☐ no

9. Do you know what the acquirer will require from each?

   ☐ yes ☐ no

10. Can you find a compromise between the acquirer and the stakeholder group?

    ☐ yes ☐ no

## Chapter 47: Sustainability of Performance

1. Do you have enough backlog prior to the sales process launching?

   ☐ yes ☐ no

2. Do you have enough pipeline prior to the sales process kicking off?

   ☐ yes ☐ no

3. Can the new business team stay focused on bringing in new clients during the sales process?

   ☐ yes ☐ no

4. Can the owner's work be delegated to other team members during the sales process?

   ☐ yes ☐ no

5. Is the forecast reliable?

   ☐ yes ☐ no

6. Will the forecast remain reliable during a time of great distraction during the sales process?

   ☐ yes ☐ no

7. Have you provided enough deal support to the finance team?

   ☐ yes ☐ no

8. Can the finance team handle the constant requests for reports?

   ☐ yes ☐ no

9. Have you reviewed examples of information memorandums?

   ☐ yes ☐ no

10. Have you attempted a practice run in putting together an information memorandum?

   ☐ yes ☐ no

## Chapter 48: Managing Interest

1. Are investors inquiring about buying your firm?

   ☐ yes ☐ no

2. Are you making a good first impression by not divulging too much information too early?

   ☐ yes ☐ no

3. Have you created the appropriate amount of competitive tension among the buyers?

   ☐ yes ☐ no

4. Do you know who the right investment banker is for you?
5. Have you hired them?

   ☐ yes ☐ no

6. Do you have a realistic, market-based price in your mind?

   ☐ yes ☐ no

7. Have you waited the appropriate amount of time before suggesting a price?

   ☐ yes ☐ no

8. Do you understand the typical deal structures for boutiques like yours?

   ☐ yes ☐ no

9. Are you prepared to engage and let prices drift up over time?

   ☐ yes ☐ no

10. Have you hired the best attorneys and accountants to complete the transaction?

    ☐ yes ☐ no

# APPENDIX B
# GLOSSARY

**Problem:** The business problem a client is trying to solve.

**Client:** The person(s) who buys, and uses, your services.

**Competitor:** A firm, or approach, similar to yours, that solves a client's problem.

**Revenue:** The income generated from providing your services.

**Service:** A service provided to a client requiring specialized knowledge or skill.

**Go-to-Market:** The approach your boutique uses to reach its clients and deliver its value proposition.

**Engagement:** A contract between a client and your boutique that specifies the work to be done, the timeline, and costs.

**Market:** A group of potential clients who share a common set of needs.

**Team:** A group of employees who work together.

**Scale Capital:** Funds used to scale your boutique.

**Leverage Ratio:** The number of nonpartners to partners.

**Cash Flow:** The money coming in and going out of the boutique.

**Life Cycle:** The series of evolutionary stages your boutique goes through over the course of its life span.

**Yield:** The measure of your boutique's productivity.

**Pricing:** The strategy a boutique uses to maximize profits by selling their services for appropriate prices.

**Replication:** The process an owner uses to eliminate himself or herself as a bottleneck.

**Culture:** How things get done at your boutique.

**Business Development:** The process your boutique uses to acquire new clients.

**Service Offering Development:** The process of bringing new service offerings to market.

**Client Experience:** How your boutique exceeds a client's expectations.

**Organizational Structure:** How your boutique's employees are arranged, including the number of employees and their roles.

**Recruiting:** How your boutique brings in new employees.

**Partner Pay:** How a partner is compensated by your boutique, including salaries and bonuses.

**Equity:** The value of the shares in your boutique, split among the various owners.

**Power:** How your boutique is governed.

**Strategy:** How your boutique wins.

**Exit:** The act of selling your boutique.

**Mistakes:** Common missteps that could cost the sale of your boutique.

**Market Position:** The strength of your value proposition relative to others.

**Growth:** A relative measure of your boutique's increasing revenue and profits.

**Client Relationships:** The primary asset of your boutique.

**Fee Quality:** A measure of a fee's ability to increase the net worth of your boutique.

**Intellectual Property:** An invention to which one owns the rights. These rights are protected by patent, copyright, or trademark.

**Sales and Marketing Process:** How your boutique acquires new clients and markets to prospective clients.

**Employee Loyalty:** The degree upon which employees are likely to stay with your boutique.

**Management Quality:** A measure of the abilities of your boutique's management team.

**Culture Fit:** How an acquirer's culture matches the culture of the boutique being acquired.

**Organizational Design:** How your boutique's organization structure impacts the sale of the business.

**Continuous Improvement:** How your boutique improves its services or manner of doing business.

**Innovation:** A new idea, service, or business model.

**Financial Market Trends:** Industry trends that may harm or help the sale of your boutique.

**Comparables:** The valuations, and terms, for boutiques similar to yours that recently sold. Also known as "comps."

**Universe of Buyers:** The number of potential buyers for your boutique.

**De-Risk:** Lowering the amount of risk present in your boutique.

**Buy versus Build:** How an acquirer determines if it is worth buying a boutique or building internally.

**Shareholder and Stakeholder Alignment:** A measure of your boutique's shareholders and stakeholders agreement in regard to selling the boutique.

**Sustainability of Performance:** Whether your boutique has been performing well up to the sale of the business.

**Managing Interest:** How your boutique responds to interest from potential buyers.

# ACKNOWLEDGMENTS

This book would not exist without the help and support of a great many people. I am glad to have the opportunity to offer my thanks to them here.

My gratitude goes to the members of Collective 54 and to our partners at Capital 54. Your stories and insights are woven throughout the book. I hope I found the right balance between protecting your privacy and sharing authentic details.

To the teams at Collective 54 and Capital 54: You allow me the freedom to create. Things I create, like this book, come to life through your hard work. Thank you.

I would also like to thank my extraordinary peers at YPO. There are too many to list, as there are close to thirty thousand members in 140 countries, many of whom allowed me to interview them for this work. Thank you.

I could not have written this book without my experiences at SBI. Starting, scaling, and selling SBI was a thrill ride. The team who went along with me on the journey holds a special place in my heart. As an expression of my gratitude, I remind you of a favorite quote from Aristotle: "To avoid criticism say nothing, do nothing, be nothing." Here is to your rapidly evolving STL.

I am also grateful to the owners, CEOs, and peers who made the time to read early copies of this book. Your enthusiastic comments added value to the work. I hope you feel that we have created something useful and meaningful.

I could not list acknowledgments without thanking my wife, the fabulous Brooke. Her constant encouragement to turn my creative exhaust into tangible things motivates me to produce. If not for her, much of what I have to say would go unheard.

# ABOUT THE AUTHOR

Greg Alexander is the chief investment officer of Capital 54, the only family office that invests exclusively in boutique professional services firms. He is also the founder of Collective 54, the only national peer network for owners of boutique professional services firms. In his work, Greg draws on his experience starting, scaling, and selling his boutique, Sales Benchmark Index. As CEO, Greg led SBI to the largest exit of its kind. This made him one of the wealthiest people in the professional services industry. The proceeds from the sale are now used to help others do what he did—reach their dreams.